# The Life of Saint Edward, King and Confessor,

## by

## Blessed Aelred,

## Abbot of Rievaulx

# The Life of Saint Edward, King and Confessor, by Blessed Aelred, Abbot of Rievaulx

## First English translation by Fr Jerome Bertram, FSA

Saint Austin Press, 1997

First printed 1990 at St. Edward's Press, Guildford
This edition copyright 1997, The Saint Austin Press.

A catalogue record for this book is available from the British
Library.

ISBN 1 901157 75 X

Printed in Great Britain by BPC Wheatons, Exeter.


The Saint Austin Press
PO Box 610
Southampton
SO14 0YY

# Acknowledgments

The author wishes to thank various members of the history faculty of Royal Holloway and Bedford New College (University of London) for advice and encouragement, and, in particular, John Doran for reading and commenting on the first draft.

The cover picture is taken from a window by Hardman's of Birmingham at St. Edward's church, Sutton Park, near Guildford, photographed by Richard Little. Illustrations in the text show details from the screen in Westminster Abbey from photographs taken for the Royal Commission on Historical Monuments (England), crown copyright, used with permission.

St Edward the Confessor is blessed by
St. Peter for aiding a cripple. (Engraving from Porter.)

# List of Contents

## Book One

7

# Book Two

Collation of the Chapters of Aelred's *Life* with those in Jerome Porter's version (Porter, 1632), the anonymous *Life* (Barlow, 1962), Osbert of Clare (Bloch, 1923), and the Bollandists (*Acta Sanctorum*, 5 Jan)

| Aelred | Porter | anon. | Osbert | Bolland |
|---|---|---|---|---|
| 1 | I | | II | I |
| 2 | I | 39v | II,III | I |
| 3 | I | 39v | III | I |
| 4 | II | 39v | III | I |
| 5 | III-IV | 39v | IV | II |
| 6 | IV | 40v | IV | II |
| 7 | V | | | II |
| 8 | VI | 54 | V | III |
| 9 | VIII | | V | III |
| 10 | IX-X | | VI-VII | IV |
| 11 | XI | | VIII | VII |
| 12 | XVI | | IX | VII |
| 13 | XII | | X | V |
| 14 | XIII-XIV | 46v | XI | VI |
| 15 | XVII | | XII | VII |
| 16 | XVIII | | XIII | VII |
| 17 | XIX | 54v | XIV | VII |
| 18 | | | XV | VII |
| 19 | | | XVI | VII |
| 20 | | | XVII | VII |
| 21 | XX | 46 | | VIII |
| 22 | XXI | 45v | | VIII |
| 23 | | | XVIII | IX |
| 24 | XXII | | * | IX |
| 25 | | 50v | XIX-XX | X |
| 26 | XXIII-XXV | | XXI | X |
| 27 | XXV | | XXII | X |
| 28 | XXVI | 52 | XXIII-XIV | XI |
| 29 | XXVII | | XXV | XI |
| 30 | XXVIII | | XXVI | XI |
| 31 | | | XXVII | XI |
| 32 | | | XXVIII | XI |
| 33 | | | XXIX | XI |
| 34 | XXIX | | XXX | XI |
| 35 | | | * | XI |
| 36 | | | | XI |
| 37 | | | | XI |
| 38 | | | | XI |
| 39 | | | | XI |

(* = found only in the Cambridge MS of Osbert)

# Translator's Introduction

When Henry II came to the throne of England he was hailed as the one who brought to an end the divisions caused by the Norman conquest, for both the Saxon and Norman royal lines met in him. To promote this new found unity, the cult of King Edward the Confessor was promoted, culminating in his canonisation in 1161. Shortly afterwards, on 13th October 1163, the new saint's body was solemnly enshrined in Westminster Abbey. Thomas Becket, Archbishop of Canterbury, presided, and several other bishops and earls attended. On this occasion the honour of preparing a sermon was given to Aelred, the revered Abbot of Rievaulx. He took as his text "No man lights a lamp to place it under a bushel", but no copy of this sermon has yet been found. On the same occasion Aelred undertook to write the Life of St Edward, and this is the text now first presented in English.

Aelred's *Life of Edward*, it must be admitted, tells us very little about the historical personage of the king. In the finest tradition of English historians, Aelred gives only one date in the entire book, and that is 1066. The work is almost all derived from the earlier history by Osbert of Clare, and should be seen as hagiography, intended to inspire the reader to piety and virtue, not as a bald account of past facts. Subsequently it became very well known, was circulated widely, and survives in a great many manuscripts. If it tells us little about Edward the man, it tells us a very great deal about later medieval devotion to St Edward, and as such is a historical source of some value. It is for this reason that it is considered worth translating and publishing, so we may distinguish the Confessor of faith from the Edward of history.

# Aelred of Rievaulx

In recent years much attention has been paid to the entrancing figure of Aelred. As one of the formative figures of the Cistercian order, a close associate of St Bernard of Clairvaux, he has attracted the attention of many writers, monastic and otherwise. New editions and translations of his spiritual works are available, and his *Spiritual Friendship* has achieved the status of a popular classic. His historical works, although perhaps more popular in his own time, have not received so much recognition.

Walter Daniel, Aelred's biographer, tells us something of the circumstances of the writing of the *Life of Edward*. Both the sermon and the life were written at the request of Lawrence, Abbot of Westminster, who was a kinsman of Aelred. The occasion was one of reconciliation, of Saxon and Norman, as well as of king and pope - it had been Aelred who had helped to persuade Henry II to recognise Alexander III as pope two years before. The frequent references to the papacy in the *Life*, as well as those to Henry II's unifying position, show Aelred's purpose. Unity and concord were to be promoted, controversy and strife banished.

Whether Aelred actually preached the sermon at Westminster Abbey in person remains doubtful. Barlow cites the *Peterborough Chronicle* which states that he was present (Barlow 1970, p. 283n) and he seems to have been a witness to a judgment at Westminster, along with Abbot Lawrence, in March 1163 (ibid, p. 284 n). On the other hand the description of the translation cited in the *Acta Sanctorum* names as present the king, the Archbishop, fourteen bishops, eight earls and four abbots, among whom Aelred does not appear. It may well be that the writer, by now an ageing and unwell man, did not attend in person but sent the text of the sermon to be declaimed by another. The introductory letter to the *Life* speaks as if Abbot Lawrence had not seen Aelred in person, but had written, enclosing a copy of Osbert's work, "which you were good enough to have delivered to me". In Daniel's life of Aelred we are told of only one further book which he wrote, and that unfinished, the treatise on the soul (Daniel, p 42). It would appear that Aelred was already gripped by the illness which Daniel tells us afflicted him for four years before his death (Daniel, p 49).

# Previous Lives of Edward

The most factual of the sources for the life of King Edward is the *Anglo-Saxon Chronicle* (Whitelock, 1961) which tells us, year by year, of the principal events of his reign. The majority of these events are omitted by the various *Lives* which were written to edify rather than to inform. The earliest, possibly written in the short reign of Harold, is the anonymous one edited by Frank Barlow (Barlow 1962) attributed to a monk of Saint Bertin. This is more interested in the person of Edith, and is loud in the praise of Godwine and all his family.

The major source for Aelred was a second *Life* written by Osbert of Clare, a monk of Westminster, in 1138 (Bloch, 1923), which became the vehicle for the first, unsuccesful, attempt to secure the king's canonisation. Osbert omits all reference to the Godwine clan, and tells many tales of miracles, including posthumous ones which helped to enhance the growing cult of Edward in Westminster. Into the text he inserts two papal bulls and a letter from the king to the pope, presumably from manuscripts preserved at Westminster.

It was Osbert's book that Aelred undertook to re-write. He improved the style enormously, changing it from a pseudo-classical encomium to a work of Christian erudition. The Godwine family reappears, but now as the villain of the story. Little genuine history remains, and the only other passages which Aelred adds to Osbert are miracle stories. Of these the famous tale of the Ring, and that of the sceptical seamstress (chapters 24 and 35) are found in one manuscript of Osbert, but appear to have been added subsequently to Aelred's work. The last four chapters are not paralleled in Osbert, but two of them relate to Osbert himself, and they may be from a lost section of his *Life*.

In an earlier work, *Genealogia Regum Anglorum*, Aelred writes briefly about each of the Saxon kings, and his short section on Edward (see Appendix) derives more from William of Malmesbury's *de Gestis Regum Anglorum*, written about 1124. Most of the material given in the Genealogia does not reappear in the full-length life, and other stories deriving from William reach Aelred filtered through Osbert.

# Aelred's *Life* and its Influence

It will be seen that the value of Aelred's *Life* is spiritual rather than historical. He stresses the virtues of the saint, his chastity, his humility, his devotion to the papacy. His wife, alone of all her family, is a paragon of virtue, seen dutifully attending her husband on his deathbed. There is no mention of his repudiation of her when she was banished to Wherwell, nor of his rejection of his mother Emma. His military exploits are also passed over in silence.

In common with Bernard and other Cistercian writers of the period, Aelred fills his text with scriptural phrases. Occasionally he adverts to this, and quotes deliberately, but most often he is using scriptural phrases, particularly from the psalms, as the most natural way of expressing himself. We must remember that as a monk he recited the entire psalter in choir every week of his life, and it would be remarkable if the language and phrasing of scripture did not become second nature to him. There is accordingly no point in italicising every biblical passage and giving references: that would make the text unreadable. I have tried to give the same effect by echoing the English version of the psalms in common use, but scriptural references have only been provided in the notes where they are significant.

In the centuries following the publication of Aelred's *Life* it was copied and circulated widely, displacing the earlier lives, and providing the basis for all later devotion to Saint Edward. The mid- fifteenth century screen to the Confessor chapel in Westminster Abbey was carved with a series of fourteen scenes taken from Aelred's *Life*, which we have been able to reproduce in this edition. The tale of the Ring in particular caught the imagination, and the saint is most often shown in art holding it. Many manuscripts of this *Life* survive, and it was first printed in the mid-seventeenth century (Twysden, 1652). Before that it had been used as the source for Dom Jerome Porter's life (Porter 1632), in which about a third of the text is translated. The Bollandists used it for their version in the *Acta Sanctorum* which abbreviates the Latin text. The full text appears finally in Migne's *Patrologia Latina* from which the present translation has been made. A critical edition was announced as part of the *Corpus Christianorum* series, but so far only the volume containing Aelred's ascetical works has appeared.

Sutton Park 1990

# The Life of Saint Edward, King and Confessor, by Blessed Aelred, Abbot of Rievaulx

## Prologue

It was, we learn, the concern of many of our forbears to write about the works and lives of the notable men who flourished in their own times, and so by their pens to perpetuate the memory of those whose happiness was already believed to be perpetual. It would moreover be in their estimation of no little benefit to later ages if those whom they might profitably imitate were rescued from obscurity. What indeed could more easily arouse and encourage the human spirit to strive for perfection than reading or hearing of those who were already perfect, to learn their way of life, and savour their renown? None could claim that something which he knows another has achieved is impossible for himself: none could doubt the reward of a good life if he reads that it has been attained. That is why our Lord and Saviour, from whom the world has received the saving Faith, wished there to be, among so many frail ones, a number of the perfect, by whose example others might be encouraged to believe, or goaded towards a holy way of life. So it has been even to our own unhappy age, when crimes abound and virtues are scarce; children are ever born to succeed their parents so that the ignorant young may be educated into their elders' knowledge, rely on their experience and be moulded by their example.

Now above all states and kingdoms on earth, England can indeed be proud of her saintly kings, for some were crowned again by martyrdom, rising from an earthly to a heavenly reign; others chose exile from their homeland, preferring to die as pilgrims for Christ; several renounced their crowns and embraced the discipline of a monastery; yet others reigned with justice and holiness and strove to be their people's servant more than lord. Among these last, that brilliant luminary the glorious King Edward shone like the morning star in a cloudy sky, like the moon at its full all his days.

It was at the urge of the worthy father Abbot Lawrence of Westminster that I, insignificant though I be, undertook to put into some sort of writing his life and notable miracles, and to dedicate the work to you, most glorious King Henry. Thus you may learn how great his merit was in the sight of God with whom he now reigns in heaven, and why our Holy Mother the Church has decreed he should now be so much more honoured on earth, now in your own time when you weild the authority of a king.

The justice of such a great king deserves imitation, and it is impressive to see his self-restraint in the midst of so much wealth and luxury. Physical descent from his saintly stock is the particular boast of our King Henry. We believe that he promised that you would be the consoler of all England, for we have come to understand that in his prophetic parable at the end of his life he was designating you, the corner stone at which the two walls, the English and Norman nations, have come together, to our great delight. But of this elsewhere!

Now, most noble King, inheritor by double right of the kingdom of such a great ancestor, commend yourself earnestly to the prayers of him, from whose father and mother alike you derive your kingdom and noble blood. Entrust yourself to his careful protection, be sure to imitate his holiness as well, and so you will achieve happiness for ever with him. Amen!

# Preface
## To Abbot Lawrence of Westminster

Brother Aelred, useless servant of the brothers who live at Rievaulx, sends the love he owes in Christ to his worthy father Lawrence, the Right Reverend Abbot of Westminster: whom he loves, whom he should love, and whom he would like to clasp to his bosom.

I am reduced to idiocy at your request. Who am I, in what way qualified, what special knowledge or style have I that you should pick on me to put into words the life of that holy man King Edward, the admiration of the ages? Can my writing commend him, can my rhetoric praise him? If a subject that Cicero might be stretched to expound is entrusted to my care, would it not result in obscurity more than illumination? Why do I imagine you have done this? Out of appreciation or out of affection? Or why not both? After all I considered both worth savouring, and so added my appreciation to yours, my affection to yours; one spurred me on and the other gave me confidence to study the volume which you were good enough to have delivered to me.

But look - I found here someone more than man: someone who "in his days pleased God and was found righteous", who was conceived of holy stock, and, not satisfied with the thirty or sixtyfold return, rose triumphantly to the hundredfold harvest of virginity. I must therefore entrust myself completely to his faith, give myself entirely to his example, rely on his help and prayers, not only because of your own sacred command, Father, but also because having examined his simple humility, and indeed conceived a real devotion to him, I have had to do the best I could.

I have poured that wine which, as Scripture says, "begets virgins", from an old flask into a new one, and if the latter is not so fine, it may well be more practical for simple people.

Although I did not depart from the account given in the original book, I have added, where I thought it would be helpful, a few points taken from the most faithful histories, or from the most reliable old traditions. I decided also to insert the letters giving the king's privilege from the Roman Pontiff, and an explanation of his dying prophecy, in such a way that you can either read them coherently in their proper place, or omit them without breaking the sense of the narrative. As a reward for my labours I request of your holy community, which under your command serves the cult of this great king, prayers and Masses for my sinful self, so that I, who have no merits to boast, may gain eternal life with the help of such a worthy confessor.

# The Life of Saint Edward
# Book One

## 1: His Nobility and Holiness

If I am to commit to writing the life of the glorious King Edward, the beloved of God, I must begin with a quotation from Saint Peter, the Prince of the Apostles. In wonder at the centurion's conversion he says: "Truly I have come to understand that God does not discriminate between peoples, but those who revere God and act justly are accepted by him, of whatever race they be." God recognises his own people, in every nation, in every walk of life: he loves anyone he wishes to love, he shows his mercy to anyone he pleases. He deploys his strength from one end of the earth to the other, and he orders everything for their good. Poverty in itself does not produce holiness, any more than do riches acquire it; obscurity does not make you perfect, and fame does not condemn you; being free does not bar the way to paradise for you, nor does lack of freedom unlock it.

Abraham, the first of the patriarchs, is described as being wealthy, as well as saintly. His faith commands our admiration as his obedience our imitation, and they are demonstrated in the midst of great material wealth. Joseph was appointed master of Egypt by the king, and his chastity was a model for the world to imitate. It was when holy Job was deprived of all his possessions that he showed what sort of man he had been when wealthy: his fame for remarkable patience was increased by his physical illness, his wife's nagging and his friends' reproaches. King David was richer and more holy than anyone, no one was more distinguished, no one more humble: he was buried among fabulous treasures, and considered more acceptable than any of God's friends. Let no one be surprised, therefore, if we call our Edward both king and saint: we shall see how he was frugal in the midst of riches, temperate when surrounded by luxury, unassuming while robed in splendour, and indifferent to worldly things while wearing a golden crown.

Surely no one else was born with such an advantage in all these matters, for he had a model of all kinds of holiness in the most saintly and worthy kings from whom he traced his physical descent. From the much renowned and most pious King Alfred, the one whom Pope Saint Leo, in Rome itself, consecrated and anointed as king over all the kings of England, he was in the sixth generation, although the tenth among those of that dynasty who succeeded to the throne. Both numbers indicate an eventual profit: in carrying out his work he was bearing most stalwartly the burden and the heat of the day, as at the sixth hour; while in the evening he received the reward of ten hours' work from our heavenly Father's largesse.

Now after Alfred, sometimes sons succeeded their fathers, sometimes brothers their brothers on the throne: eventually all the happiness and holiness of all the others seem to have been concentrated in King Edgar, who excelled them all in holiness as in renown and splendour. When he was born they say the angels sang, and promised peace in his lifetime for the Angles. It was for this reason that he acquired the name of peacemaker, which he shared with Solomon, both because of the heavenly presage and that presage's effect: a name which promised a reign progressing in peace, as indeed it was.

His son was the forceful King Ethelred, who married Emma, daughter of Richard the noble Duke of Normandy. In this way a more holy offspring was guaranteed by the double holiness of both parents. For the reputation of the illustrious Dukes of Normandy, Richard, brother of this Queen, and Robert her nephew, is established by their admirable lives and their deaths no less distinguished. Our Edward was born of these ancestors, and enhanced the dignity of his birth by his wisdom and conduct. But now it is time to examine how his holiness first arose, how it developed, and to what end; I shall describe them with my pen for the inspiration of many.

The Nobility of England swear fealty to Edward
before his birth.

# 2: How before he was born he was chosen to be King

The great King Ethelred had begotten two sons, Edmund, known as Ironside, by the daughter of the well known Earl Thoret, and Alfred, by Emma, his queen, but the blessed Edward was preferred to both of these while still in his mother's womb. This was the work of God, who does all things according to his choice and design, and governs human royalty, which he gives to whomsoever he pleases.

There was a grand assembly of bishops and lords in the king's presence, as well as a great gathering of the commons, and since there were already sad presages of a coming conflict, they were discussing the succession to the throne. The king, therefore, who wanted to nominate his own successor, enquired what each and every one had to say. The issue was undecided, since everyone had different opinions. Some considered that Edmund should be preferred to the others because of his outstanding physical strength: others thought it would be more diplomatic to choose Alfred because of the influence of his Norman blood. Yet God who knows all that is to come, foreknowing the short life of the former and the early death of the latter, swayed the votes of all towards the child not yet born. Still in the womb, he was chosen to be king: the unborn outranked the born, he who had not yet touched the ground was named the lord of the land. The king agreed to the choice, the nobility gladly took their oath of allegiance, and, remarkable to relate, swore fealty to one of whose birth they were still unsure.

This was your doing, O Jesus Christ, for you govern all things everywhere; you indicated by these signs that this man should be ruler of your people, for you had chosen him and loved him before the world was founded. Although you worked through men, it was not they but you who made the choice. It is obvious indeed that it was unprecedented, inappropriate for that time, contrary to reason and against all common sense to pass over legitimate grown-up sons and, while an enemy attack threatened, to choose as king a child not yet born, who could command neither the terror of the enemy nor the respect of his subjects in a time of such emergency. It was Almighty God who sent a spirit of prophecy on the votes and loyalties of his people, moderating present woes with the hope of future prosperity. So all recognised that this king would be a comfort to the whole kingdom, and no one doubted that, although the people did not understand what was happening, he had been chosen by God himself.

.

The Birth of St. Edward. (Westminster Abbey)

# 3: How he was exiled to Normandy with his mother

The blessed child was born, washed at once with the waters of baptism, and confirmed with holy chrism to be more closely united to Christ. He became the temple of the Holy Spirit, and in the service of that Spirit he was brought up.

A little later the Vikings invaded England, and by burning and killing devastated most of the island. The queen and her children were sent across to Normandy, so that the king could be free from the anxiety of such a great responsibility, and so be the more courageous in repelling or capturing the enemy. Sure that his wife and children were safe, he had no fears that any harm could come to them, whatever the outcome.

The child Edward grew and became strong, and the Lord was with him and guided all he did. The boy lived among the boys of his grandfather's house, but was preserved from the vices which adolescence and human nature usually develop. The child behaved with the dignity and maturity of an adult: he kept his body chaste, his conversation restrained, his actions straightforward, his affections pure. His unusual kindness and cheerful helpfulness won the affection of all his peers.

Already at that age he enjoyed attending church, giving frequent time to prayer and assisting at solemn High Mass. He was eager to visit monasteries where he knew he would find friendship among monks of great holiness: two of these became his special friends, and are said to have appeared to him as he was dying, as we shall hear later.

# 4: How a certain Bishop at Glastonbury had a revelation about him and his reign

In the meantime the enemy power was ravaging England, killing and plundering everywhere. Cries of desolation resounded in all quarters, churches were set on fire, monasteries sacked, and, as the Scriptures say, "They have poured out the blood of your Holy ones around Jerusalem, no one was left to bury the dead." Priests abandoned their charges, and took refuge in monasteries or remote places where some little peace and rest might be found, there to bewail the misery of many.

Among these was the reverend man Brithwald, Bishop of Winchester, who came sad and grief stricken to the monastery at Glastonbury, to give time to prayer and the Office. He was on one occasion praying with tears for the deliverance of the kingdom and its people, and broke out in these words: "How long, O Lord, how long will you turn your face away and forget our poverty and oppression? They have slaughtered your holy ones, overthrown your altars, and there is no one to set us free or protect us. I know, O Lord, I do know that everything you have done to us was truly just, but will God continue for ever to afflict us, and never grant that easier times may come? O Lord, my God, will there be never an end to these terrors? Will your sword rage against us for ever, and strike us till all are dead?"

Worn out with grief and prayer, he fell into a soothing sleep. In a dream he saw the choirs of heaven all lit up, and the great saint Peter sitting on a high throne, dressed as his exalted dignity required. In front of him he saw a man of noble aspect, handsome and dressed in royal splendour. The apostle with his own hands consecrated this man and anointed him king. He gave him prudent counsel and urged him in particular to virginity, telling him besides how many years he should reign.

The bishop was amazed at this remarkable sign, and asked

the saint to explain to him the secret of this vision, begging a prophecy from the apostle also on the future of the kingdom and the ending of the present distress. The saint, with a kindly expression, looked into his eyes: "The kingdom is the Lord's," he said, "the Lord's, O bishop. He is the one who governs the children of men. He it is who distributes royalty and appoints authorities. Because of the sins of the people he gives power to the unworthy. Your people have sinned indeed against the Lord, and so he has handed them over to the enemy, and those who hate them have power over them. But God does not forget his mercy, nor is his kindness obscured by anger. So it shall be, when you are asleep with your fathers, buried after a respected old age, the Lord will visit his people and bless his inheritance. He will choose himself a man according to his own heart, who will carry out all his wishes. With my assistance he will claim the throne of England and put an end to the ravages of the Danes. He will be one acceptable to God and pleasing to men, loved by his subjects, a terror to his enemies, a support to the Church. And when he has finished the determined span of his reign in justice and peace, he will make a holy end to his admirable life."

All these things were shown in the event to have happened to the blessed Edward. The bemused bishop turned back, weeping, to his prayers. He realised that he would not live to see the happiness of his people, but he was no less delighted at the certainty that their woes would have an end, and poured out thanks to God. Thus he was consoled, and was able to preach repentance to the people, promising them constantly that God's mercy would not fail them.

# 5: How his reign began and of his brother and nephews

The tempest raged on, its violence unabated: civil strife piled on external threats till no one knew whom to trust, to whom to confide his secret thoughts. The island was crawling with spies; no one's confidence was safe, no one's loyalty beyond doubt, no one's words unguarded. At length so great was the treachery of the natives and the cunning of the invaders that after the death of the king and the exclusion of his lawful heirs, the greater part of the island surrendered to Cnut. The valiant King Edmund was slain, the heir to his father's greatness and his own; his children still in the nursery were delivered to the Vikings for slaughter.

Once all was under Cnut's control, he made a closer alliance with the Duke of Normandy by taking as his wife Emma, the widow of the late King Ethelred: he was afraid that a legitimate heir might seek the kingdom which was his by right, relying on the strength of the Normans. A little later Alfred, Edward's brother, crossed to England to see his mother, and was put to death by his enemies and fellow citizens with unimaginable cruelty. Edward, destitute of all human assistance, lived in exile from his homeland, though not from justice. Deprived of his kingdom, he preserved his faith, stripped of his honour but not his merit.

He was wary of the wiles of the wicked, and knew them too well by experience: he lived in fear lest his own people, bribed by the enemy, should betray him to death. But he found sage counsel in laying himself habitually before God, bewailing his isolation in such words as these: "See, O Lord, I cannot assist myself: those whom I need have abandoned me. My friends and neighbours have turned against me, and maintain their stance. My father, after so many trials, has passed beyond human cares; my brothers have fallen to cruel murderers; my nephews driven into exile; my mother, handed over to marry our rival, has made my enemy victorious. I am the only one left, and they seek my life.

"But if I in my poverty am abandoned, it is into your hands, O Lord: you will aid your orphan charge. Long ago when Edwin, the noblest of our family, was exposed to death, you saved his life and his kingship. You brought Saint Oswald, England's glory, to the throne out of exile, and by the sign of the cross you gave him power over his foes. If you therefore will be with me, if you will protect me, if you will bring me back to my father's throne, you will be ever my God, Saint Peter the Apostle ever my patron. I vow that I shall visit his holy relics, in the city where he and his fellow apostle lie, with your kind guidance, you ever at my side."

So he prayed, and arose stronger in faith, more eager in hope, a happy man waiting confidently on the Lord, and his confidence was not misplaced. Cnut was taken beyond human cares; his sons carried off by early deaths, the English liberated fron the heel of the Danes like Israel from Egypt, and blessed Edward was chosen as king. Once before the whole island had sworn allegiance to him, before he was born: now they welcomed him to England with the greatest honours and universal rejoicing. The Archbishops of Canterbury and York together with almost all the bishops of England anointed him, and he was consecrated as king.

What glory then was England's! What joy for all the people when they saw their ancient liberty restored! Without hope they had lamented: in Edward they found what they had lost: peace for the people, honour for the nobles, freedom for the Church. The sun dawned again, the moon shone brightly, when Edward was crowned with splendour and might. The priests were examples of holiness and wisdom; monasteries burgeoned with regular observance; the clergy fulfilled their charge, the people took their proper place. Even the land seemed more fertile, the air more pure, the sun more sultry, the sea more serene. For when a peacemaking king reigns long enough, all nature converges in a bond of peace: no infection remains in the air, no turbulence in the sea, no barrenness in the earth, no disorder among the clergy, no unrest among the people.

The rumour of such well-being, at his accession to the throne, reached neighbouring kingdoms too. Kings and princes were swept off their feet with wonder at such a change of affairs: they were eager to strike a treaty with such a great king, to make an alliance with him or to establish peace. The Roman Emperor's cousin had married Edward's nephew, the son of Edmund Ironside (one of the two whom Cnut had ordered into exile), and so the emperor was delighted at our king's good fortune, and sent an embassy to make a closer treaty of friendship. The King of France, a near relation by blood, became nearer yet in the security of peace. It was thus said of the blessed Edward as Scripture said of Solomon: "All the kings of the earth desired to see his face and hear his wisdom!" Only Denmark continued to threaten a murderous attack on England and the slaughter of her people: we shall see in the event what came of such an attempt!

St. Edward is consecrated as King. (Westminster Abbey.)

# 6: Of his admirable behaviour and manners

In the midst of all this, our saint was not puffed up with human pride, but acknowledged God's profound goodness towards himself, pondering well on the sage's words, "Have they made you prince? Be not proud but remain among them as one of them." He set himself this manner of life: to treat his servants as equals, but the priests with humility, to be popular with the commons, sympathetic to the unfortunate, generous to those in need. His devotion to divine worship was remarkable, as was his concern for building or reconstructing churches and monasteries. He made no distinction between persons, but judged the poor with equity and pleaded with justice for the lowly of the land: the king might be exalted on his throne, decked with purple and gold, but he was nonetheless a father for the orphan and a champion for the widow.

His treasury seemed to be the common property of all: a public fund for the poor, since the king considered all that he had to be not his own, but everybody's. He gave to all who asked, but kept silent about his income. He was shy of receiving, glad to give. He never forgot a gift, and was eager to give in return.

His body itself was illuminated by his inner spirit of holiness, and you could see in his face an unusual mildness, dignity in his walk, straightforwardness in his affection. His conversation combined authority and humour, seasoned by the names of Christ and his Blessed Mother. He could be awe-inspiring or comforting, instructive or cheering. None ever saw him conceited, out of temper or the worse for overeating. He might indeed be unintentionally deluded into excess through his natural innocence and openness to others, but he never knowingly and deliberately gave way to anger or illicit desire. There is no need to praise his modesty, which he retained constantly, the comfort of his exile, the standby in his adversity, the companion of his good fortune.

He was moreover unnaturally indifferent to money, seeming neither distressed at its loss nor glad at its acquisition. We can give you an example of this virtue of his, to illustrate his remarkable openness and equanimity as well as his unassailable good temper. This story became well known throughout England, leaving some to wonder at his naïvety, others to praise him as a saint.

# 7: How a thief plundered his treasury under his very eyes

The king was once resting, lying on a couch, but some concern prevented him sleeping, as often happened. A chamberlain came to the chest in which the king's money was kept, and took out or put back whatever the occasion demanded. He then left to continue his duties, forgetting to close the chest. A small penniless boy noticed this - they say he had been sent in to collect the plates off the table - and he came to the chest, pulled out a considerable number of coins and stuffed them inside his tunic. He left, and hid them somewhere he thought would be safe for the time being. Then he returned and repeated his crime, while the king watched. The third time he tried it, the king spoke: he was, I believe, inwardly aware that the guardian of the treasure was approaching, and wanted to spare the boy any danger. "You are being careless, boy," he said. "Take my advice: secure what you have and escape, since, by Our Lady, if Hugelin comes he won't leave you a single coin." (Hugelin was the name of the royal chamberlain.)

The boy escaped, and the king neither betrayed him nor pursued him. The thief had hardly taken to his heels when the chamberlain returned, and was astounded to see the royal treasury diminished. He went pale, and trembled, his sighs and shouts showed his distress and anger. The king rose, and, as if unaware of what had happened, asked why he was so disturbed. The chamberlain informed him, and he replied "Be calm; perhaps the one who took it needed it more than we: let him keep it, we have enough with what remains."

Now I ask you, was any king more just, any one more ingenuous? How could any one be so meek as to watch himself being robbed and keep silence, indeed even warn the thief to be careful? I consider that this simplicity and tolerance, to let the thief keep what he took, is a greater virtue than his healing the blind, curing the lame, or rescuing many from misfortune. And so, having considered it profitable to insert this story, let us return to our narrative.

St. Edward watches the thief plundering his treasury.
(Westminster Abbey.)

# 8: Of his chaste marriage, of his own and his queen's virginity

When Edward was secure on his throne, and peace and prosperity were well established, the nobles, anxious about the succession, advised the king to think about marriage. The king was struck with fear that by the heats of passion the treasure he kept in an earthen vessel might be lost. But what to do? If he refused stubbornly, he was afraid that the secret of his pious resolve might be betrayed: if he agreed to their pressure, he dreaded the shipwreck of his chastity. Finally, as they insisted, in season and out of season, he judged it safest to yield, and commended his modesty to the Lord in these words:

"O Good Jesu, your mercy once preserved three boys unscathed in the Babylonian furnace. By your aid Joseph kept his chastity, leaving his cloak with the wicked libertine. The noble Susanna, supported by your aid, vindicated her virtue against the libidinous priests. Holy Judith preserved the city from seige through her singular chastity, which was neither shaken nor even tempted among the royal banquets and brimming cups of Holophernes: her woman's hand was strengthened to strike off the wicked man's head. And far above all these, you willed that unique hope of the world, our most dear Lady, your Mother, to be both spouse and virgin, nor did the sacrament of matrimony bring an end to her virginity. See, I your servant, the son of your maidservant, striving as I can to love you and your dear mother, am not so presumptuous as to aspire to equality with your majesty, but with trembling I hope for some semblance of such greatness. Come to my aid, therefore, O my Lord, son of my virgin Lady: O my Lady, Virgin and Mother of my Lord: help me to undertake the sacrament of marriage in such a way as not to endanger my chastity."

The king accordingly agreed to the will of his nobles, and

search was made for a maiden whose honourable birth and virtuous life might make her fit for such a king's embrace. The most powerful of all the magnates of England was Earl Godwine, a man of great wealth and singular acuteness; he was a traitor to both king and kingdom, but so skilful a deceiver and so prompt in dissimulation that he could easily sway the people to agree to whichever party he wished. But Godwine begat Edith, as a thorn does a rose: she might indeed derive her body from him, but her majestic holiness flowed from the Holy Spirit. She it was that Christ prepared for his beloved Edward, inspiring her from childhood with a desire for chastity, hatred of vice and love of virtue.

While still a girl she displayed the dignity of an old woman, and shy of company preferred to haunt her private chamber. She was not accustomed to dissolute laziness, nor laborious work, but passed her time in reading and manual tasks, embroidering clothes with amazing skill, interweaving gold with silk and representing any sort of natural object: with such peaceful employment she avoided vice and the attentions of young men. She was beautiful enough in appearance, but more so in her upright way of life. Godwine therefore designed to bind the king to a closer friendship, which had been strained by his murder of his brother and frequent betrayal, and worked on his friends in the royal court to propose his daughter as a bride for the king. Those also who were much closer in affection to their master considered this to be most essential for the king, for they were well accustomed to the earl's treachery, and feared him all the more.

So it came about that for opposite reasons, everyone agreed on one proposal. Both sides contributed their wealth for the marriage feast; the bishops performed the sacrament, and the girl was blessed as a wife and crowned as a queen. The king and queen, once united, agreed to preserve their chastity, without feeling the need to invoke any witness other than God to this pact. She was a wife in heart, but not in flesh: he a husband in name, not in deed. Their conjugal affection remained, without their conjugal rights, and their affectionate embraces did not rupture her chaste virginity. He loved, but was not weakened; she was beloved but untouched, and like a second Abishag warmed the king with her love but did not dissipate him with lust; she bowed to his will, but did not arouse his desires.

Let not anyone disparage this story of the king's virtue, but know that at that time it was told and believed throughout England, as was certified by those who were sure of the fact, and more who knew of their intentions. There were indeed some, whose thoughts rose no higher than flesh and blood, who believed that it was out of weakness that the king had been compelled to marry into a treacherous family, and that he withheld his conjugal duty lest he produce more traitors. Yet this opinion is easily refuted, when you consider what love they had for each other. I thought I should mention this so that it may be known that no one at that time doubted the king's continence, though they might dispute the reason for it. His pure mind bears sure witness to the king's chastity, for serenely free from all vile desires, with detachment he could regard both the present and the future, seeing distant things as if before his eyes, as the following chapter will declare.

# 9: How he observed in the Spirit when the King of Denmark was drowned in the providence of God

There came that festival which commemorates the day when the Spirit of the Lord filled the whole world, to renew the face of the earth, and divine flames lit upon the disciples to cleanse their minds, flames which enlightened them with wisdom, softened them with grace and hardened them for martyrdom. On that day the blessed king assisted devoutly at divine worship; outwardly he was adorned with his noble sceptre, his splendid robes and royal crown, inwardly he considered the glory of all these to be no more than dung, but he wore them conscientiously for their sacred meaning. All the nobles of England were there, their robes embroidered with pearls set in gold; giving all the honour they could to the sacred dignity of the day, and the majesty of the king.

During the celebration of Holy Mass offered in the church of St Peter, the king was totally recollected and put aside all earthly concerns for spiritual ones. He was praying earnestly, and while the sacrifice was offered for the general welfare, the intentions of his own prayers were grace for himself, peace for the people and pardon for all. Suddenly, at the moment when the spiritual gifts were being distributed to the congregation, the king's face brightened, his eyes lifted, and, while preserving the dignity of a king, he dissolved into quiet laughter.

The bystanders were amazed, and no wonder: this was not the sort of thing they had been used to see in him. When everything was done that was considered apt to celebrate such a great day, those who had noticed it asked him to explain to them why he had laughed. He, being simplicity itself, simply answered their simple question. "The Danes and their king", he said, "were determined to renew their ancient crimes, and disrupt the peace which God had graciously bestowed on us. When we were being worsted it was a punishment which came on us from the Lord, but they in their ignorance of God's justice, boasted of their own strength, saying "It was our hands that prevailed: the Lord had no part in this work". For as God had been angry with our ancestors and given us over into the Danish power, they attributed this to their own strength, and imagined that they could easily do the same now, being unaware that he who strikes also heals, he who brings death brings also life, he who leads down to hell also brings up again.

"The Danish king, therefore, gathering his army together, today ordered his ships prepared, since the winds were favourable to his design. They were bringing supplies and weapons on board, the sailors got the weapons ready while the soldiers took their alloted places. The ships were all ready to set sail, the sails spreading to the wind, when, at the time my face shone, the wicked king, too haughty to support himself, stumbled and slipped to his knees: he had carelessly overstepped himself, and fell from the prow: the deep closed over him, the waters covered his head. Thus he opened a trap for us and dug it deep, and in the trap he had made he himself fell. The Lord struck the head of a wicked house and cursed his sceptre, and the whole of his army which was approaching like a hurricane for our destruction. But, as when the head is cut off all the limbs lie still, so when their prince was drowned, the evil force was scattered. I place my hope in the Lord my God and in his blessed Mother, that in my time none of their efforts will be brought to completion. This is what I saw through Christ's revelation: I saw it, I laughed and was glad. The Lord it was who made me laugh, and whoever hears it will laugh with me."

The time and hour were noted: messengers were sent to Denmark to make careful enquiry about everything, and they found that all had happened at the exact time that heaven had revealed it to the saintly king. The report of a miracle of such magnitude struck fear into the hearts of all who heard it. They acknowledged that God was fighting for Edward, and not only the Danes but other nations as well sent ambassadors and gifts to sue with him for peace.

The King of Denmark is drowned in a shipping accident.
(Westminster Abbey.)

# 10: He speaks to the Nobles of the Realm of performing his Vow: Messengers are sent to Rome.

In times of prosperity, the saintly king never forgot his vow, and in days of happiness remembered his former sorrows. Pondering again what great things were done for him by the Lord who enriches the poor, lifts up the lowly and crowns the humble, the king got ready to fulfil the vow which his lips had uttered. He collected his expenses, set money aside for gifts, and calling the mighty of the whole kingdom, he discoursed to them as follows on the state of the realm and his own pilgrimage:

"Blessed be God whose mercy towards us is ever greater; he visits our iniquities with the rod and our sins with the scourge, but he has not taken away his love from us. Look: he casts down the mighty from their thrones, and has exalted the humble and meek: the hungry he has filled with good things, and the rich he has sent empty away. Kings rule through me, he says, and princes discern justice. We have not forgotten how the barbarians had invaded our inheritance, we were made a rebuke to our neighbours, a mockery and a scorn to those who surround us. For they left my family no honour, no glory remaining; some they had killed, others driven into exile, others oppressed with the yoke of shameful slavery. At last, when my father was dead, my brothers slain, my nephews exiled, when fortune favoured our enemies in all things, there seemed to be no hope at all that I would succeed. Yet I, believing and hoping against hope, and surrendering myself to the Lord's mercy, made a vow to make my pilgrimage to the thresholds of the holy apostles, and thenceforth committed myself to God's protection and providence.

"God looked on my prayer, did not disdain my petition, and took away my reproach. He restored me to the kingdom of my father, and added to that both riches and honour, as well as filling me with heavenly gifts. It was he who subdued my foes, without shedding of blood, he overthrew my enemies and settled all our affairs in peace and goodwill. Never let us be found ungrateful for such favours: rather, since we have been liberated from the power of our enemies, let us serve God with justice and in truth.

"Let us do as the prophet said: 'Pay your vows to the Lord'. Help me to make provision for the safety of this realm of England while I am on pilgrimage; with what peaceful laws and justice all should be administered, who should be in charge of which region, who should look after the castles, the cities, the public and the private good. God will be the one who guards and protects all, he will preserve the peace he has given, he will travel with me and remain with you, will protect you and bring me safely home."

When he said this the whole assembly shuddered; tears and sighs betrayed their inner dismay. The hand of the Danes, withheld through his merits, was still daily feared, and they were terrified of the total ruin of their country. The populace came to hear of it, and there followed protests and riots, the island awash with tears as if the fires were burning already. You could see the poor now holding their hands up to heaven, now falling again to the ground; their thoughts were but of graves and burial, as if they would all die of hunger as soon as the king departed. Then all together protested against the king, insisting that they should not be deserted, not be exposed to violence, that the country should not be handed over to its foes, the pledge of peace which God had granted should not be surrendered, in short that for one supposed good so many dangers should not be incurred.

The bishops fulminated, the nobles pleaded, the people demanded, that the journey should be, if not cancelled altogether, at least deferred. The king, sensitive to the urging of so many tears, cries and prayers, wavered long between duty and desire, considering it as perilous to break a vow as it was inhuman to refuse to yeild to such prayers and entreaties. At last, wishing to discover from God what was best, he decided provisionally to defer the pilgrimage, rather than abandon it, and so have time to consult the wishes and advice of the Holy See, and accept her decision whether to commute or perform the vow.

When they heard this, both rich and poor rejoiced so much that you might think their Edward had a second time been restored to them, recalled anew from exile. Everyone did what suited their station, office or ability so that the king should not tire of the delay: some offered prayers, others almsgiving, while several offered to go on pilgrimage in his place. Envoys to the Holy See were quickly chosen: Aldred, Archbishop of York, Hereman, Bishop of Winchester, two abbots renowned for religious observance, and several others, both clergy and laymen. Their needs were provided for, and they set off for Rome with the king's authority.

Surely it must have been in God's providence that the royal messengers found a major synod gathered there, at which Pope Leo of happy memory presided to discuss the affairs of the church. This distinguished gathering of holy men was glad at their arrival, and they in turn took the presence of so many bishops as a sign of heaven's blessing on their mission. It was, they considered, a great grace from God that such men were collected from the ends of the earth for such an assembly at that time.

At the urging of the Holy Father the messengers accordingly expounded the reason for which they came, and the assembled fathers listened attentively in silence. They explained the king's wishes, the dangers to the kingdom, the risk to peace, the cries of the poor and the tears of orphans; they told their fears of how the scab which had formed over England's recent wound, inflicted by Danish spite, might be broken open if the king were absent.

When the envoys had finished, all voices were raised in thanks and praise, extolling the king's love of God, and the people's love of the king. They were amazed to see the mildness of David and the wisdom of Joseph combined with the riches of Solomon in one prince. Finally the Pope gave his opinion, and all agreed together, that for the quiet of the realm, the good of the Church, the needs of the poor and the peace of monastic life, the king should be solemnly absolved from the bonds of his vow through the authority of God and Saint Peter and the sacred synod then assembled, and that the expenses he had collected for the journey should be given to the poor. In compensation for the vow a monastery should be built, or one destroyed by the barbarians rebuilt, at the king's expense in honour of Saint Peter.

The ambassadors accordingly offered the gifts which the holy king had directed to the churches of the saints, and they received the Pope's blessing before joyfully seeking their home with the apostolic letter. They crossed the sea and delivered the letter at a meeting of the council which the king had called for that purpose.

# Papal rescript

*LEO, Bishop, Servant of the Servants of God, to Our Beloved Son EDWARD, King of the English, Greetings and Apostolic Benediction!*

*Inasmuch as we have learnt of your laudable desire which is pleasing to God, we give thanks to him through whom kings rule and princes decree justice. Whereas the Lord is close in every place to those who cry to him in truth, and the holy apostles conjoined with their head form one spirit, and equally hear the prayers of the faithful; and moreover inasmuch as it is agreed that your departure would be perilous for England for it is you who restrain the stirrings of rebellion by the bridle of justice; by the authority of God and the holy apostles and the sacred synod, we do absolve you from the burden of this vow by which you fear to offend God, and from all your sins of omission and commission; relying on that power which the Lord granted to us in blessed Peter, saying "Whatsoever you shall loose on earth shall be loosed in heaven." Therefore we command you in the name of holy obedience and penitence, that you shall distribute to the poor the funds which you have gathered for this journey, and you shall either construct anew a monastery in honour of Saint Peter, Prince of the Apostles, or increase and repair one now decayed; and you shall establish a sufficient income for the brothers out of your own revenues, inasmuch as they may praise God there devotedly and the glory of the saints and your own merits be alike increased. Whatever you shall grant to that place, or shall be otherwise granted or conferred we confirm and establish by our apostolic authority, so that it shall always be an abode of monks and shall not be subjected to any layman, save the king. Whatsoever privileges you shall think fit to establish there pertaining to the honour of God we do grant and confirm with our supreme authority, and we do condemn those who infringe them with an eternal malediction.*

# 11: Of a Vision which appeared to a certain Recluse about the King

There came a revelation from heaven concerning the king's marriage and the Pope's letter, for the Prince of the Apostles appeared to a holy man, who knew nothing of what was happening in Rome, when the messengers were not long on their way. This man was beloved of God and mankind: he had lived for many years enclosed in an underground cavern and was now close to the reward of his labours.

The blessed Peter stood by him in a dream, and by his mild voice and countenance dispelled his fear. "Edward the king", he said, "has decided to consult the Church of Rome about the vow which he undertook when still in exile, and also about the peace of the realm and the government of the people, being concerned for the needs and demands of the poor. He will come to know that he is absolved of his vow by my authority, and he will receive instructions from the Pope about a monastery to be constructed in honour of my name. Let him not hesitate to trust the apostolic letter, follow its instructions and agree with its advice. For the message originated from me, since he chose me once as his patron, companion and minister of grace.

"There is a place West of London, selected by me and beloved: once I consecrated it with my own hands, dignified it with my presence, and made it famous for divine miracles. Thorney is the name of the place, and for the sins of its inhabitants it was long since handed over to the pagans. From a wealthy place it has become poor: from fame it has declined to obscurity, from honour to contempt. Let the King undertake to repair this place, under my authority, to be a dwelling for monks: let the buildings be restored, the revenues increased. This shall be none other than the house of God and the gate of heaven. There a ladder shall be erected, by which angels can ascend and descend carrying the prayers and vows of men to God, and bringing grace in return. I shall keep the gates of paradise open for those who ascend from there, and, through the office which my Lord and Saviour laid on me, I shall untie the fettered, receive the forgiven, and open the gates of a heavenly fatherland to those once bound by their sins and now justified.

"Your task is to write down all that you can remember of what I have said and be sure to send to the king. He will thus be found more ready to love and obey me through receiving God's message through two channels, more confident in his absolution, more eager to carry out the command."

Having said this, the vision disappeared with the light. The hermit, with no delay, got a skilful scribe to set down in writing what he had seen and heard. He handed the letter to a runner, and directed him, as he had been instructed, to the court, which was many miles away. And so it happened that on the same day, in the same place and at the same council convened to receive the envoys back from Rome to deliver the apostolic command, the letter of the holy man was presented to the King and made public. The letter of Pope Saint Leo was read out, and immediately afterwards was delivered the message from the holy old man.

With voices raised and hearts afire they blessed God for his gifts and praised him for all his works. All wondered at the king's holiness and rejoiced in the apostle's glory. They were strengthened in their faith, their hopes lifted from earthly to heavenly concerns, their love of God more profoundly inflamed. There could be no hesitation about the truth of the message, since there was no way that a man in Worcestershire, withdrawn from human society, could know what was happening in Rome, what commands the envoys had received and when they would return, had it not been revealed by God.

The king, joyful and triumphant, dispersed and gave to the poor the money which he had collected to sustain him on pilgrimage, as he had been commanded. He emptied his treasuries as he applied himself to the appointed task. Moreover he remitted, by royal bounty, the heavy tax which in his father's time had first been levied for the Danish fleet, and was afterwards brought every year to the royal treasury: this intolerable burden was forever lifted from England. Hence it is not inappropriate to adapt for our holy king the scripture: "Happy the man who is found without stain, who goes not after gold nor places his trust in a well-filled treasury." He was "found without stain" because of his chastity. He "went not after gold" but rather gave it away. He "put no trust in his treasury" since he not so much diminished as extinguished it in God's cause.

Who is this man, that we should praise him? He has done wonderful things in his lifetime, restoring sight to the blind, steps to the lame; dispersing fevers, healing the paralytic and curing the different ills of mankind. We have thought it fitting to gather and record here examples of these things.

The levying of the Dane-gelt which Edward remitted.
(Westminster Abbey.)

47

# 12: Of the cripple whom the King cured by carrying him

It happened that, when the king was living at peace in the royal capital, in the palace near St Peter's abbey, he met an unfortunate man, of Irish origin, called Gillie Michael in his own language, who was deprived of the use of both feet. His hamstrings were so contracted that his legs were bent back against his body, the heels pressed against his haunches so that his ankles were sunk into the flesh and rendered his whole body useless from the waist down. He crept along, with hands towards the ground, supported by crutches, and dragged his body along, groaning under his own weight: a pitiful sight to those who witnessed it, one which stirred many to charity.

To add to the weight of his woes, he was extremely poor, so that lack of food and the inclemency of the weather combined to leave his body shrunken with consumption and starvation. So it was, then, that he crept into the court, and presented himself to the royal chamberlain: "Look, Hugolin", he said, "can't you see me? Are you not sympathetic? Are you not moved by so much suffering in one man?"

"What would you like me to do?" he replied.

"Six times," said the poor man, "have I visited the thresholds of the holy apostles where they lie in Rome, crawling there in the way you can see, but I have not yet gained my health. Yet Saint Peter has not denied but only delayed my prayer, since he wished blessed Edward to be his ally in this miracle, knowing that he is entirely devoted to him. Now I am about to set off the seventh time for Rome, and I have received a command from the holy apostle to seek out the king, and to convey to him the apostle's wish that he should carry me, on his holy back, to the church which is near the palace, and that if he did that I should receive a total healing of my limbs through his merits."

This was conveyed to the king, who gave thanks to God, and promised that he would obey the apostle; he would not fail the poor man but would carry out the commands that he had received. The sick man was told, and came at once. The king, as strong as the ass in the Gospels, got onto all fours and offered his shoulders to carry him. Hear this, all ye nations, give heed, all who dwell on the earth! Gather round to watch a circus never staged before, a display without parallel! The beggar, in all his squalor, hung on the shoulders of the great king, and wrapped his loathly hands and scaly arms around the king's chest and neck. What a necklace, more splendid than jewels! What a tiara, more precious than gold, brighter than electrum!

Of the bystanders, some just laughed; others taunted the king for being taken in by the beggar, others thought the just man's simplicity and meekness were sheer folly. See: a new David dancing and leaping, and a new Michal jeering and laughing! But those of sounder sense considered him happier under his strange burden than under a golden crown. For it was you, O Christ Jesus, you who were being carried in the beggar's person, just as when Martin clothed the poor man, you were clothed. On that former occasion you revealed yourself in words, now by a miracle.

For when the king had advanced a little, charged with his honourable burden, suddenly the nerves which had been contracted by that long standing illness were relaxed: the flow of blood, which had been obstructed by the tightness of his veins, was renewed; the bones grew strong, the withered flesh made whole. His ankles emerged from the flesh, his feet were detached from the haunches. The man stretched his legs, his knees now flexible, and the poison gushed out with blood to adorn rather than defile the king's robe. Everyone now cried that the man had been sufficiently healed, and that the king should now relinquish his burden, because of the filthy sores. But he, remembering his orders, turned a deaf ear to the sirens' song, and entered the church to deposit the sacrifice he was bringing to God and Saint Peter in front of the sacred altar.

The sacristan of the church, a man of great piety named Godric, lifted the poor man off the saint's shoulders, washed his limbs, now cured of their sores, and sent him away soon after, sound and whole. The man stood on his own feet, soles and heels made firm, and was presented to the king, who gave him provision for his journey. So, blessing God, he set off for Rome, to give thanks to Saint Peter, and to proclaim the holy king's virtues everywhere. The crutches, on which he had depended to crawl miserably along, were hung in the church as a witness to this great miracle: a pleasing sight for the observers, and evidence of the king's holiness to all who entered.

This miracle gave the holy king an even greater incentive to love and revere Saint Peter, and it inspired him with a desire to conclude the work which he had begun in his name, firing him with love. Above all other places consecrated to Saint Peter throughout England, this one in particular was chosen for restoration, for he had learnt that it was of all others most dear to the saint, not only through the heavenly vision we have already described, but also through the record of much more ancient miracles. Though it may seem irrelevant, we shall insert them into our story to illustrate the king's interest in this work.

# 13: Of the Church at Westminster Dedicated by Saint Peter

When King Ethelbert was ruler of Kent, and received the holy sacraments at the preaching of Saint Augustine, his nephew Sebert reigned over the East Anglians, and accepted the faith through the mission of the same bishop. He constructed a church in honour of Saint Paul within the walls of London, which he made the capital of his kingdom, and wished to be a major episcopal see. Saint Mellitus was its bishop, whom saint Gregory had sent with several others to assist Augustine, and who was the best of them in merit and pontifical dignity.

The king, wishing to ingratiate himself with both Apostles, founded a noble monastery in honour of Saint Peter, outside the walls of the same city on the western side: he dignified it with many gifts and rich possessions. The time arrived when the church there was ready for dedication, and everything necessary was prepared for the place, the occasion and the community. The bishop was staying the night in a tent, getting ready for the next day. The people were eager with anticipation, for being still young in the faith, they enjoyed being present at solemnities not only for devotion but also for entertainment.

On that very night the blessed apostle Peter appeared dressed as a traveller to a certain fisherman on the further bank of the river Thames, which flowed by the said monastery; he offered his fare, and asked for a passage across, which he was granted. Stepping out of the boat he entered the church, as the fisherman watched - and lo, suddenly a heavenly light shone, and all was illuminated with amazing splendour, turning night into day. There accompanied the apostle a multitude of the heavenly host, passing in and out, and a heavenly anthem resounded from a choir in procession. All was full of light, all suffused with joy. Hearing was enhanced with the glad song of angels; scent sated with an ineffable fragance; sight dazzled with the radiance of heaven.

Earth and heaven seemed conjoined; the human linked to the divine, and angels were seen as on Jacob's ladder ascending and descending throughout the sacred ceremony. What then? When all the ceremonies fitting to dedicate a church had been carried out, the great fisher of men returned to the fisher of fish. He found him terrified, dazzled by the divine light, and all but senseless. With consoling words he brought the man to himself and calmed his mind again. The two fishermen entered the skiff together, and the apostle spoke to the man using the same words his master had once used to him: "Have you anything to eat?"

"I have caught nothing," he replied, "for I was so overcome by the brilliance of the strange light, and moreover delayed waiting for you, but I was confidently expecting the fare you promised me."

The Apostle replied: "Now let down your nets for a catch."

The fisherman did as he was bade, and soon the net was full of a great quantity of fish. He got these to the shore, and the Apostle said "Take this fish, which exceeds all others in size and worth, to Bishop Mellitus from me. The remainder keep for yourself as the fare for my passage. I who speak to you am Peter, who with my fellow citizens have dedicated this church built in my honour, and by the authority of my holiness have forestalled the bishop's blessing. Tell the prelate therefore what you have seen and heard, and the marks made on the walls will be evidence of your statement. Let him not, therefore, continue with the dedication but only supply what I have omitted, namely the most holy Mysteries of the Lord's Body and Blood: let him edify the people with a sermon, and strengthen them with a blessing, and make it widely known that I shall frequently visit this place, and here shall attend to the vows and prayers of the faithful. For those who live sober, just and holy lives in this place I shall keep open the gates of heaven."

Having said this, the keybearer of heaven vanished. Now already dawn was bringing the night's darkness to an end when the fisherman, with his fish, ran up to Saint Mellitus as he was processing to celebrate Mass for the coming dedication. When he had told all to the bishop, everything turned out as the apostle had said. The prelate was astounded, on opening the doors of the sacred basilica, to see the pavement inscribed with the letters of both alphabets, the walls anointed with oil in the twelve places of consecration, as many candle-ends adhering to the twelve crosses, and everything still damp as if recently sprinkled.

There could remain no further doubt in anyone's mind about what the fisherman had related, since these heavenly tokens witnessed to his statement. The bishop relayed this to the people, and soon with one voice they stormed heaven, praising God and blessing him who, to strengthen the faith of all, had made of our heavenly and earthly fatherlands a single commonwealth for the dedication of this most holy church. They believed in the miracle, and all the descendants of that fisherman never failed to give a tithe to Saint Peter and his servants of all the profit which their trade brought them thenceforth, as their father had instructed them. Only one of them once dared to defraud them, and he soon lost the use of his skill until he admitted his guilt, brought back what was due, and promised amendment.

# 14: Of the reply sent to the Pope by the holy King

When Saint Edward had discovered this story, through tradition and ancient records, his heart blazed within him, and he became ardent in his intention to dignify that monastery yet more with buildings, decorations, rights and property. In order that these should remain secure, whole and sacrosanct throughout future ages, he entrusted everything to the authority of the Holy See for ratification. For he was always unsure of himself, always aware of his own frailty; despite the frequent miracles which glorified him daily, and the delights of peace which he enjoyed, he was firmly established on the rock of humility. Happy indeed is the man who fears the Lord, who takes delight in all his commands. Indeed glory and riches are in his house, his justice stands firm for ever.

He had newly been freed from his vow by apostolic authority: now, still concerned about it, he prepared to send messengers again to the apostolic threshold, once again to consult the apostolic majesty, once again to ask for the same or another compensation for his vow to be enjoined upon him. Other problems also had emerged for the English Church, on which the primal see was to be consulted, that of which it was specifically said "the gates of hell shall not prevail against it." So the holy king, in his concern for the common good, wished all to be done according to the norms of the Catholic faith, and desired that everything be correct so that his own salvation might be ensured and others might receive the apostolic teaching for their salvation. Along with Aldred, Archbishop of York, two others were sent who had been elected bishops, Giso for the church of Wells, and Walter for that of Hereford.

These two, in the presence of the archbishop with whom they travelled, received the rite of consecration from the Pope himself; they took their places with honour among the other fathers at the council which happened to be in session (at God's will as I think) in the Lateran Palace. When a suitable moment occurred, they produced the king's letter, and added the other commissions he had given them. The opinion of the supreme pontiff was one with those of the whole sacred assembly, in favour of the holy king, as was right. The envoys received a letter from the Holy Father, and with no untoward incident in their journey, regained the king and their homeland with great alacrity.

# The King's Letter to Pope Nicholas

*To NICHOLAS, Supreme Father of the Universal Church, from EDWARD, by the grace of God King of England, all due submission and obedience!*

*We give glory to God that he has taken care of his chosen Church, in appointing you as an excellent successor to your worthy predecessor. Therefore we consider it right to apply to you, as to a solid rock, both to ratify our own good actions, and to have your approval and association in the good work, inasmuch as you may renew and increase for us the grants and privileges which we obtained from your predecessor; that is to say that the command he laid on us in the name of obedience and penitence because of the vow which I swore to visit Rome, and for the remission of all my sins, to build a monastery in honour of Saint Peter, should be ratified by you, and that you should confirm, renew and increase the privileged property and rights of the said place, and decree that they should remain inviolate for ever. I myself for my part do increase and confirm the gifts and pecuniary customs which Saint Peter holds in England, and I send these collected monies with royal gifts to you, that you should pray for me and the peace of my kingdom, and establish a continual and solemn commemoration of the whole English people before the bodies of the holy apostles.*

# The Privilege of the Lord Pope Nicholas

*NICHOLAS, Bishop, Servant of the Servants of God, to our most glorious and religious son, distinguished and worthy of all honour, EDWARD, King of the English, graces of all kinds, a saving consolation and apostolic blessing!*

*We give thanks to Almighty God, who has in all things adorned and inspired your most excellent majesty towards Peter, Prince of the Apostles, to seek friendship with us, and to acquiesce in all the apostolic decrees. We are therefore sending your nobility a letter, associating with it the company of the saints, the apostles and ourselves, praying for the mercy of him who is Lord of all and King alone above all, that he may make you a sharer of whatever good works we or our brethren may have before God, and make us associates in love more and more as time passes, and firmly establish no less a part of our authority in your kingdom than we hope to have for ourselves. We have indeed been most constantly praying for you, doubt it not, that God may subject to you all enemies and foes who may wish to rise against you, and confirm you on your father's throne and rightful inheritance, and may Saint Peter be a guide and helper for you in all adversity!*

*For it is well known that the Kings of the English, for the reverence and devotion which they displayed towards the blessed Apostle Peter, have prospered with renown and dignity, and gained famous victories for their nation. Through the merits of the same blessed apostle, may God give effect to your wishes and desires, and strengthen your rule over your father's kingdom, granting it increase, and after this life has run its course, lead you to an eternal kingdom of everlasting glory.*

*We therefore do renew, confirm and augment your privileges: that is to say that you are absolved from the vow that troubles you, and from all your other sins and iniquities, by the authority of Him who wished me, unworthy though I be, to preside over his Church. Moreover, concerning that place which you have undertaken to reconstruct and improve for the sake of holy penance, since, as it* appears, it received its first consecration of old from the blessed Apostle Peter, whose unworthy vicar we be, and since it was an ancient royal seat, by the authority of God and the holy Apostles and this Holy Roman See, and our own, we do concede, permit and most certainly ratify that it should be for ever a greater monastery, consecrated and royally founded, to be a depository for the crown jewels, a dwelling place of monks for ever, to be subject to no person save the king, and that they shall have the right to choose suitable abbots in succession to govern the place according to the Rule of Saint Benedict, nor shall any outside person be intruded by force, but only those that the assembled community chooses to rule over them.

Therefore we do absolve that place from all dues and episcopal domination, so that no bishop shall enter therein to confer ordination or give any order, except by the consent and at the request of the abbot and monks. Let the said place have a free enclosure, that is the surrounding land including a cemetary for the dead without any respect or toll due to any bishop or anyone else. Moreover gladly and with a joyful heart we to the extent of our authority do grant all the things which pertain to the freedom and dignity of the same place, to the glory of God. The properties which ancient kings, or any other men, you yourself and your nobles, have granted to that place, and the charters made about them, we confirm with the divine authority and our own, we decree them to be ratified and established.

We do condemn with the eternal malediction of the traitor Judas all who shall infringe, appropriate, diminish, disperse or sell such properties, that they shall have no part in the happy resurrection, but know that they shall be judged by the blessed Apostle Peter when he sits with his fellow Apostles to judge the twelve tribes of Israel. To you, therefore, and your royal posterity we commit the patronage and advowson of the same place, and of all the churches of all England, so that representing us you may establish what is right in consultation with the bishops and abbots. By this you shall know that you are to receive a just reward from him whose reign and empire will not fail nor be lessened in *eternity!*

When he had read these gems of apostolic majesty, the holy king exulted for joy, and put off all the anxiety which he had suffered over his vow; committing all the business of the kingdom to his peers and nobles, he dedicated himself totally to the divine service. Yet the more he withdrew from corporeal things, the more brilliantly he gave himself to spiritual studies. Thenceforth he merited to be consoled yet more by frequent revelations of heavenly secrets, as shall be declared in what follows.

Christ appears to St. Edward and Earl Leofric at Mass.
(Westminster Abbey.)

# 15: How he and one companion saw Jesus in the Sacrament of the Altar

Our most Christian monarch used to attend the holy mysteries of our Redemption at the altar dedicated in honour of the Holy Trinity in the monastery of the blessed apostle Peter, which he had undertaken to rebuild and augment. It happened that Earl Leofric was also present, who had a reputation for complete reverence and mildness of spirit; his memory is held blessed. His wife was called Godgifu, who complemented the meaning of her name with splendid practical action, for the name means "good gift". Maybe Christ brought her to be a good gift to the Church, or maybe she offered herself as a most gratifying present to God through her faith and devotion. So it was with such a companion at his side that the saintly earl, ever attentive to the work of God, was the founder of many monasteries, and lived soberly, justly and religiously in all things, naming Christ as the heir to his property and wealth.

This man then stood a little removed from the king's side, worthy in every way to witness and testify to such a great miracle. The heavenly rite was being performed at the altar, and the sacred elements were held in the priest's hands. And lo, the fairest of the children of men, Christ Jesus himself, appeared visibly to the eyes of both; he was seated on the altar, and held his sacred right hand over the king to sketch the sign of the Holy Cross in blessing. The king bowed his head, and worshipped the presence of the divine majesty, showing his reverence for such a blessing by his bodily demeanour. The earl, ignorant of what the king was thinking, but wanting to share in the king's great vision, felt a desire to go to him. The king, knowing well what the earl intended, said "Stay, Leofric, stay still; I see the same sight as you!" Then turning to prayers and tears, they were overcome with the glory of God's house, and drank from the stream of his delight.

When Mass was over, they spoke together about the heavenly vision, nourished by the bread of heaven: "day unto day took up the story". The king frequently interrupted by sobs, said: "O my Leofric, I beseech you by the majesty of him we have seen, let no rumour of this reach the public as long as we live, lest popular acclaim bring us through pride to destruction, or the malice of the incredulous undermine trust in our words." In this he followed his Master's example, who when he had been transfigured before his disciples, said as they came down the mountain, "Tell no one of the vision until the Son of Man has risen from the dead."

The earl left the court, prompted by divine inspiration, as I believe, and kept his master's command in such a way that later generations were not deprived of the story of such great holiness. For he came to the monastery at Worcester, and told the story to a certain monk in confession, binding him with the same promise the king had laid on him. He asked him to write down the great secret of the vision, and deposit it in a secure place, so that the present generation might be ignorant, but future ones come to know of it. The holy man agreed to this petition, and concealed the requested account of the vision in a casket of holy relics.

A long time had passed after the holy king's death before the casket was found, at God's prompting, as I believe; it was open, though by no human hand. While the brethren were carefully investigating the saint's relics, they found the scroll and unrolled it. Unwilling to conceal such a treasure, they read it out to all the people. In this way, that which the king wanted concealed was revealed by God's providence, so that the king's humility was attested, but at the same time the faith of believers was strengthened by the revelation of the miracle.

# 16: Of the tumours and worms expelled from a woman by the King's touch.

After this miracles increased, and signs multiplied: the hand of the Almighty was stretched out further to proclaim the king's merits. There was a young woman, newly married, who suffered from two sorrows: her face was disfigured by disease, and she had lost her husband's love through her inability to conceive. Below her throat grew two tumours which deformed her whole face by their growth; under the skin the tissues rotted, turning her blood into poison, till worms appeared, emitting a horrible stench.

This disease disgusted her husband, whose love was lost by her sterility. The wretched women lived on, hateful to her husband and burdensome to her family. Few even of her friends came to her, because of the stench: rarely did she see her husband because of his revulsion. Hence her grief, her tears, her sighs by night and day, while her barrenness brought her contempt, her disease rejection. Medical care was prevented by her poverty. What was the poor woman to do? What remained save to beg the help of God despairing of human aid, as if she were to cry with the prayer of that other equally unfortunate woman, "I beseech you, Lord, to free me from the restraint of this reproach, or else to take me from this life."

In a dream she was told to go to the palace, in the hope of healing at the king's hands. If she were washed, touched, blessed by them, she could receive her health through his merits. The woman awoke, and forgetting both modesty and her illness, ran into the court, thrust herself on the king's attention, told him the message and begged his help. He was overcome by piety, as usual, and neither feared infection nor shrank from the stench. Water was brought, and he washed the parts of her body affected by the disease with his own hands, feeling the tumorous places with his fingers, and marking them with the sign of the cross.

What more to say? At once the skin broke, worms gushed out with the infection, the swelling subsided, the pain disappeared. Bystanders marvelled that such holiness should be found in a king, such power lie in the hands that wielded a sceptre. The woman remained a few days at court, while the king's officials tended her needs, until scars formed over the wounds and she could return safely to her home. Moreover, lest anything be wanting to the king's glory and the poor woman's happiness, the barren woman was given a fertility she had not hoped for, and enriched by the longed-for fruit of her womb, she easily regained her husband's affections.

# 17: Of the Blind Man healed by being washed with his hands

We learn from the teaching of Saint Paul that there are different gifts of grace, and not everyone receives all of them, for he says "Some are given a word of wisdom through the Spirit, others a word of knowledge by the same Spirit, others faith, others the grace of healing". While it was the gift of healing that our most Christian king received in special abundance from the Spirit of God, he was particularly distinguished by the special grace of giving sight to the blind, because, as it was believed, of his inner purity. As his unusual chastity kept the gaze of his heart clear, just so did he dispel darkness from the outward eyes of others.

There was a blind man, well known among the people, who had for a long time bewailed the loss of his sight, till it pleased the Saviour by a single miracle both to declare the king's virtue and to remedy the poor man's distress. The wretch was told in a dream that he would regain his lost sight through the king's merits, if he washed his face in the same water as the king. Led by the hand, he came to the palace and related his vision to the chamberlains.

They passed this on to their pious prince, who was astounded, and very indignant. He declared that the man had been deceived by some phantasy, that nothing of this sort could be hoped for from a sinner, this was an apostle's privilege; in any case no attention should be paid to dreams. They responded that trust in dreams should not be disparaged, since Joseph and Daniel had learned of the future through visions of the night, and Christ's foster-father had been warned to flee with the boy, and return again, through an angel appearing in dreams. They added that God, ruler of all, is capable of bringing help to the wretched how he wills, when he wills, to whom he wills and through whom he wills. Man has no right to refuse the divine command, nor to deny anyone the remedy which God has provided.

The king's mind wavered for a time between humility and devotion, lest his humility be lessened by yielding to their request, or his piety fail to fulfil its duty. The hour came when the king was to proceed to the church for the solemn vigil of All Saints, and as was his custom, he washed his hands. The water was caught in a bowl, and while the king was attending the holy sacrifice of the Mass, the blind man was summoned, they poured the water over his eyes, washed his face, and prayed that divine power would work through the merits of the holy king. Amazingly, as if a new Siloam had flowed from the king's hands for us, when he opened his eyes he saw the light, and blinking in the unaccustomed glare of the sun he looked all around, rejoicing as if the world were newly created for him.

Tears flowed for very joy, and the sound of thanks and praise rang in the mouths of the bystanders. The fellow entered the oratory to give thanks to God, and joined in divine worship with the others. They saw him but did not recognise him; some said that it was he, while others claimed it was not so, but only one who looked like him: he testified that it was truly he. One looked at another, one conferred with another, and the Mass ended in a hiss of whispers.

As he came out of the church the king was met by his ministers. He heard about the miracle, and turned back to the church, calling the man to him.

"Fellow" he said, "Can you truly see?"

"Truly, my Lord King." he answered.

"Can you see what I am doing?"

"My Lord, you are holding your dear hand towards me."

"And now what?"

"You are crossing your forefinger and middle finger, and pretending to threaten my eyes." the poor man replied.

"Now tell me, a third time, describe what I am doing."

"You are pulling your beard."

Then the saint collapsed in tears before the holy altar, giving thanks, and ascribing all to God, not himself, repeating after the Psalmist, "Not to us, Lord, not to us, but to Your name be the glory."

# 18: Of another Blind Man similarly enlightened by the Saint

What had been done by a person so eminent, in such a time and such a place, could not be hidden; moreover the man whose sight had been restored lived on for a long time, supported by the king at court. The story was widely reported that through the water which had washed the King's hands a man had been relieved from the darkness of his eyes. England was glad to be ruled not so much by a king as by a prophet, one who cured diseases and foretold the future, who ruled the earth with justice and the peoples in fairness.

There was a certain man in the city of Lincoln who had lost his sight through accident or disease, which deprived him of the joy of life, and left him sunk in sorrow. For three years he had been walking in darkness, until the rumour of such virtue brought him hope of regaining his health. As if chiding himself he exclaimed "Why should I hesitate? There is a prophet in England, and I am blind. I sit in darkness, in darkness do I walk, and near me shines the light of a new holiness, a king distinguished by the virtues of an apostle."

It happened that the man fell asleep while pondering this, and in a vision at night was promised a swift healing, if he were to seek out the medicine which had cured the blind man, and invoke it on himself. With no more delay, the man hastened to court, and begged the chamberlains to grant him what he desired, which they did. He washed his face with the health-giving water, and straightway the light he longed for dispelled his longtime darkness. The fellow gave thanks, and returned again to his country, declaring the king's sanctity, bringing back not only healing but great joy.

## 19: Of a Blind Man similarly healed by the King's touch

It happened that a royal palace was being constructed in a place named Brill. A sizeable band of rustics was sent to cut wood by the foremen of the work. After their labours they ate and were satisfied, and dispersed here and there into the shade to rest their tired limbs, for the noonday sun was uncomfortably hot. A little later, while the others were hurrying back to their appointed work, a lad called Wulfwine woke up and when he opened his eyes could see nothing. The poor boy turned his head this way and that, rubbed his face with his hand, wiped his eyes with his fingers, but could not dispel the darkness. At last he realised that he had lost his sight, and bursting into tears and cries, soon summoned his companions and told them what had happened.

They offered what consolation they could in his misfortune, and led him by the hand to his home. For nineteen years he "sat in darkness and in the shadow of death", and was pitied by all. But one day a good woman came to comfort him, as he wretchedly bewailed his mischance; she was a respectable woman who did much good. She asked him how he was, as people generally do, and he told her his state of mind. She replied: "I have been sent to you to bring you good advice, and if you follow it without any hesitation, your lost sight will be soon restored, your darkness dispelled."

The man began to leap for joy, and promised more than his strength warranted, but the woman gave him this answer: "My friend, go barefoot and without a shirt to visit eighty churches, there to ask the prayers of the saints with all humility; then, with genuine faith, sure hope and a glad soul, take yourself to the palace to receive your former health at the king's hands."

He made no delay, asked for a guide, and visited the churches as commanded; then full of confidence he entered the court and asked someone to introduce him to the monarch. But everyone was tired of so many people coming, and they ignored the poor man's pleas, in fact they went so far as to tell him to be quiet. He, imitating the blind man in the gospels, cried aloud all the more. The courtiers were at last overcome by his persistence in knocking, and referred his case to the king.

The king was by now well accustomed to this task. "Let him come," he said. "Who am I to sadden people when I could make them glad, if God's love can bring the promised help to a poor man at my hands, however unworthy?" The man who had lost his sight was called, and the king dipped his fingers in water and stroked his face. Then he made the sign of the cross over his darkened eyes. The grace of the Saviour acted at once, and under the king's hands blood flowed copiously from both eyes, the pupils cleared, and the swollen lids subsided.

Thus was the man restored to sight: he faced the king and looked at him. "My Lord King," he said, "I can see you, and your face is to me as the face of an angel standing before me." The king gave thanks to God, and appointed him to be a guard at the royal palace near Saint Peter's church as long as he lived. He lived into the time of William the Conqueror, a witness to the virtue of Edward.

# 20: Of three Blind Men and a One-eyed man given sight by the saint

These things are marvellous enough, but more marvels are to come! In front of the palace door were discovered four men, with but one eye between them. For the one-eyed man walked in front of three who were totally blind, and was faithful enough in little things to merit a considerable reward.

One of the courtiers was moved to pity at so many suffering from one calamity, and since he had witnessed so much virtue proceeding from the king's hands, he surreptitiously abstracted some of the water that had restored sight to the blind: his piety made him confident, trusting that as he had seen the water so publicly and powerfully working on one man, it might be as effective for many.

This faithful man came out to the beggars, and bade them trust in the Lord, and believe that their health would be restored by the holy king's merits. Then he produced the bowl and washed the darkened faces of the poor men, signed them with his thumb, and prayed that God would look not on his own merits but on those of Saint Edward. The hand of the Lord was at once manifest, and the sight they desired was restored to their opened eyes. Night was turned into day for them, and their darkened faces were dazzled by the rays of the sun. In this way seven lamps shone in the brows of four men, and made our Edward more renowned for future ages.

I have written enough for the moment about the blind being restored to sight, so let this last tale of the miracle of seven eyes teach us how the holy king was filled with the grace of the sevenfold spirit. The spirit of the fear of the Lord opened his eyes to humility and drove away the darkness of pride; the spirit of piety washed away the blindness of unbelief and poured the light of faith into him; the spirit of knowledge drove away the darkness of error and made him shine with the light of truth; the spirit of fortitude made him stronger than all his enemies both temporal and spiritual; the spirit of counsel dispelled clouds of ignorance and gave him the light of discernment; the spirit of understanding brought him from earthly things to heavenly, from physical to spiritual, from the night of this world to the contemplation of the lights of heaven; and the spirit of wisdom fortified him with the grace of prophetic insight and knowledge of the divine will. It was in short fitting that he filled the outward eyes of men with a sevenfold light, driving out their darkness, for he had deserved to be inwardly enlightened by the seven lights which are seen in the expanse of the heavens.

St. Edward cures a group of blind men.
(Westminster Abbey.)

# 21: What the King foretold of the two Sons of Earl Godwine

Now with the help of God's grace, let us tell something of the heavenly secrets about the future that were revealed to him. The holy king was seated at table one day, and Earl Godwine, the queen's father, at his side - we have mentioned him before. In front of them were his two sons, Harold and Tostig, both still boys. They were playing, but one of them attacked the other more viciously than sportsmanship warranted, and the game became a fight. Now Harold made a stronger onslaught on his brother, seized his hair with both hands, dragged him to the ground, and would have throttled him with his greater strength, had he not been quickly rescued.

The king turned to the earl. "Do you see no more, my Godwine," he said, "than a mere game or wrestle between these boys?"

"Nothing more, my Lord King," he replied.

"My mind tells me something very different, and to me this struggle reveals the future of these boys. For when they shall both have finished their childish years and arrived at manhood, hatred shall inflame the heart of each against the other; at first they shall seem to be playing with each other, by private plotting and scheming, but finally the stronger will drive out the weaker, and overthrow him when he rebels; the death of the first will be swiftly avenged by a disaster overtaking the second."

That all these things happened, all England can witness. For Tostig was exiled by Harold, and when the latter soon after succeeded Edward in the kingdom, Tostig allied himself with Harold Hardrada, King of Norway, and invaded England with a large fleet and copious army to fight against his brother. Harold engaged them in battle and emerged the victor: Tostig fell in battle, while the King of Norway fled in fear and escaped in one ship with a few followers. But in the same year Harold himself was deprived of the kingdom of England, and either died wretchedly or, as some think, escaped to live a life of penitence.

St. Edward and Earl Godwine at table.
(Westminster Abbey.)

# 22 Of the miserable death of Earl Godwine

Since we have mentioned Godwine again, I think I ought to insert the tale of how the vengeful anger of divine judgement destroyed him, who had grown rich on the profits of his treachery. In the sight of the people he received the punishment he deserved for the abominable crimes which he had committed against the king and his brother.

For he, taking advantage of the king's innocence, worked as hard as he could against justice and right in the kingdom, and often tried to pervert the king into agreeing with his wickedness. His cunning reached such a pitch that by deceit, falsehood and deviousness he had alienated the loyalty of virtually all the king's relations and friends, those whom he had brought or invited from Normandy, both bishops and clerics of other rank, and layfolk: he believed that once the king was stripped of the necessary support of his friends, he would follow Godwine's advice alone, and all would come about as he desired.

Edward, however, kept his own counsel, awaiting the right time and place, and devoted himself to God's service. He declared that God's justice would punish the great malice of the nobleman, and occasionally even said as much to Godwine himself. One day, on a popular festival, the king was sitting at the royal table in Godwine's presence, and while they ate one of the waiters stumbled carelessly against some obstacle and very nearly fell, but bringing his other foot neatly forward, he regained his poise with no ill result. Several people remarked on this among themselves, congratulating him for bringing one foot to the aid of the other: the earl as if joking added: "So it is when a brother aids a brother, and one helps the other in his needs."

The king replied: "So would my brother have helped me, if

74

Godwine here had permitted."

Godwine was afraid when he heard this, and showed a sad enough face. "I know, my king, I know that you still accuse me of your brother's death, and you do not yet disbelieve those who call me a traitor to him and to you; but God knows all secrets and will judge. Let him make this morsel which I hold in my hand pass down my throat and leave me unharmed if I am innocent, responsible neither for betraying you nor for your brother's murder."

He said this, placed the morsel in his mouth, and swallowed it half way down his throat. He tried to swallow it further, and was unable: he tried to reject it, but it stuck firm. Soon the passage to his lungs was blocked, his eyes turned up, his limbs stiffened. The king watched him die in misery, and realising that divine judgement had come upon him, called to the bystanders: "Take this dog out", he said. Godwine's sons ran in, removed him from under the table and brought him to a bedroom, where soon afterwards he made an end fitting for such a traitor.

The Seven Sleepers of Ephesus.(Westminster Abbey.)

## 23: What the Lord in the spirit revealed to him about the Seven Sleepers

I am lost in admiration as I ponder why he should merit a greater gift of spiritual insight at a time when he was more ostentatious in his royal authority, more authoritarian when surrounded by his nobles, more generous (as those who attended deemed) in lavish banquets: but man looks at appearances, God sees into the heart. Certainly he carried a sword, but it was his duty. He enjoyed royal pomp, but that was part of the sacrament of kingship. He walked about accompanied by a numerous guard, but that was out of necessity. He took the first place at banquets, but that was what was expected of him. He was lucky to be able to use all these things without abusing them, to give his body over to earthly concerns while his spirit communed with heaven.

So it happened that on the day of the Lord's Resurrection he was dressed in his imperial robes, the sceptre in his right hand, his head adorned with the crown. He had already been nourished with the flesh of the Lamb of God, and was coming to the royal table, to be restored with a meal more spiritual than carnal. For he was careful, I think, lest the groaning board, the festivities and the splendid ceremonial should even slightly draw down his mind which was intent on heaven: he was more recollected than usual, putting himself in the presence of God, and considered all these earthly things to be as dross, when suddenly his face became brighter than normal, and his inward joy bent his lips into a smile before he resumed his accustomed dignity again, and his face appeared more serene.

Those who stood or sat nearby were puzzled, and although they were in no doubt from what had happened that some secret had been divinely revealed to the king, none of them dared to ask him what it was that had occurred. When the meal was over at last and the tables cleared, the saintly king entered his solar to take off the crown jewels. Earl Harold followed him, accompanied by a bishop and an abbot, and accosted the king on this matter.

"Happy the man," said the king, " who has placed his trust in the Lord, and has not gone over to the rebels who follow false gods. The more someone withdraws himself from vanities, the more closely he clings to the truth. See, I remembered the Lord my God as I poured out my soul though surrounded by brimming cups, rich dishes and the splendour of precious metal. While I restrained my stomach, the inner eye of my mind was filled with a special light, and carried off with wonderful speed to the city of Ephesus. My gaze travelled on to Mount Celion, and lighted on the Seven holy Sleepers resting in their cave, seeing very clearly the dignity of their faces, the size of their limbs, the quality of their clothing.

"While I was watching them my heart was refreshed with the joy that my smile indicated, till suddenly in my sight they turned over, by divine power, from the right side on which they had slept for many centuries onto the left. This changing from side to side portended dire things for mankind. For henceforth, as the Gospel says, 'nations shall rise against nations, and kingdoms against kingdoms: there will be plagues and famines and earthquakes here and there.' For the next seventy years, which is as long as they shall lie on their left sides, the Lord will punish the wickedness of his people, handing them over to the hands of the gentiles till their enemies become their oppressors. For the enemies of Christ's name will attack the Christians, slaves will rebel against their masters, kings will plot against kings and princes against princes, and the sword which avenges Christ's suffering will ravage all nations."

All who heard him speak were struck dumb, and asked who the Seven Sleepers were and from what place, since in their ignorance of the world they had never heard of them: the king told them the tale of their lives, their names, their suffering and their sleeping. When they had heard this, they determined to leave evidence so that future generations might ascertain the truth of the message. The earl decided to inform the army, the bishop the clergy, the abbot the monks, and the king to send a letter to the Emperor of Constantinople.

The messengers arrived at the imperial capital, and were honourably received by the emperor. When the letters were read, his heart was filled with joy, and he was especially glad that the treasures of Greece had been revealed by God to the English. He sent to Ephesus, and by imperial command the bishop, with the clergy and people carrying incense, led the envoys into the cave, and showed them the faces and clothing of the holy ones, and that they were lying on their left sides. Then a great fear fell upon them as they saw on the martyrs in Greece all the signs which the holy king in England had told them, at the urging of the Spirit of God. They made their prayer and offered their gifts, and returned home without mishap. The Greeks were glad that what they had seen and heard agreed with the envoys' message, while the envoys themselves reported to the king and people alike this unprecedented miracle, most worthy of belief.

The king's prophecy was not in vain, for after he himself had gone to heaven, all the kingdoms of earth were disturbed. Syria was overrun by the infidel, monasteries were destroyed, churches torn down to their foundations; everywhere there were deaths, the kings of the Greeks, Romans, Franks and English were slain, and other kingdoms in disarray. It is clear that the holy king was much endowed with the grace of the spirit of prophecy, for at the same time he saw what had happened in the past, present events were not hidden from him, and the future was no less revealed.

St. Edward gives his ring to the disguised St. John.

(Westminster Abbey.)

# 24: Of the Ring which the saintly King gave to Saint John the Evangelist and how he received it back.

The king meanwhile was advancing in age and preparing to receive the reward of his labours: day by day he grew in love for God and his holy Mother, and in devotion to God's saints, among whom he venerated the blessed Peter as his special patron, and attached himself with great emotion to the disciple Jesus loved, because of his remarkable gift of chastity.

Both he considered equal in God's eyes, since one had been entrusted by Christ with primacy over the whole Church, the other privileged with a greater degree of affectionate love. Affection made up for what the latter lacked in primacy while the dignity conferred recompensed the former for his lesser love. Hence it was fitting that both were called by Christ at the same time, both were together on the mountain with Christ, both were sent to make ready the Passover for Christ in the lavishly prepared upper room; both ran together to the tomb to enquire on the resurrection of Christ, both went up to the temple at the midday hour of prayer when the lame man was healed.

Who could be happier than this apostle, who drank wisdom from the bosom of Jesus - from his breasts indeed; who was nourished on the milk of his affection? Saint Edward meditated carefully on these and similar considerations, and loved this friend of Jesus especially, after the prince of the Apostles himself. He gladly attended worship in his honour, he spoke frequently of his excellence, meditated frequently on his virginity.

It happened that a church had been built in honour of this apostle, and was being consecrated to God under that title. The king presided at the dedication, and joyfully attended the divine office out of respect for the evangelist. When he was

St. John returns the ring to the pilgrims in Palestine. (Westminster Abbey.)

The returning pilgrims restore the ring to St. Edward. (Westminster Abbey.)

walking in procession, surrounded by a numerous guard, suddenly someone dressed as a pilgrim shouted to the king, begging that he be given some alms for the love of Saint John.

The king put his hand at once into his purse, but he had already dispensed all that it had contained in similar good works. The pilgrim insisted and begged all the more. The king called for his treasurer, but he could not be found because of the crowd. The saint was much distressed, and wondered what to do. At length he remembered the ring that was about his finger, pulled it off at once and offered it to the pilgrim. The latter thanked him for such generosity, and moved off, or rather disappeared.

Later it happened that two men were making their way to Jerusalem to venerate the Sepulchre of the Saviour. One day they wandered off the public road and followed back lanes until as the sun set it grew dark, the day had ended and the men were uncertain of what they were to do or where they had got to. They stood still and debated what had happened to them, till they noticed a crowd of young men dressed in white approaching. Two candles were carried in front of them, which lit up the night to an astonishing extent. Behind this escort, and flanked by two men, came a dignified elder with white hair. His remarkably gentle face and natural poise conferred presence on him, and increased his attractiveness.

He looked at the young men and paused a while. "My dear friends," he said, "Who are you and where do you come from? Which is your nation, your king, your constitution? What is the occasion of your pilgrimage?"

"Our native land is England," they replied, "our King Edward. We follow the Christian laws, and have set out to visit the scenes of the Lord's sacred Passion and Resurrection. But today we have accidentally lost our companions, and to tell your reverence the truth, we do not know at all where we are, where to find lodging or who will show us any human decency."

The old man smiled, his face benign, and he looked them in

the eyes. "Follow me", he said, "and the Lord will look after you, for he grants all that we need."

They thanked him, and followed the old man until they reached a most imposing city. They entered an inn, the table was laid, and they ate sumptuously and relaxed. In the morning the old man accompanied them out, and when they had left the city he spoke to them as follows:

"Dear brothers, have no doubts that you will reach your homes in all safety, for the God of our salvation will make your journey easy, and I will keep an eye on you throughout the whole of your journey, for love of your king. I am John, the Apostle and Evangelist, the disciple whom Jesus loved. I hold your king in great affection for the sake of his chastity, and I would ask you to greet him from me. Lest he doubt what you say, return to him this ring which he gave me when I appeared dressed as a pilgrim at the dedication of my church, and inform him the day of his passing is approaching: within six months I will come to visit him, and together we shall follow the Lamb wherever he goes, as is fitting for one of such integrity, such bodily purity and decent way of life."

No sooner had he finished speaking than the men found themselves in the place they were searching for. They returned eagerly to their homeland, and presented the ring back to the king, telling him their message, and in private expounded what they had heard about the king's death. The king burst into tears at once when they mentioned John's name, and when he had made careful enquiry about all that they had seen and heard, he dismissed the messengers with gratitude.

# 25: Of the King's illness and the dedication of his Abbey at Westminster

Saint Edward, profiting from this revelation, knew of his death long before its event, and so, before setting out for his eternal fatherland, he was careful to send suitable messengers in advance, prayers, that is to say, and repentance. With increased generosity he dispersed his wealth, making himself friends with the mammon of iniquity, who would receive him into the tents of eternity. He wished also to see before his death the dedication of the basilica of Saint Peter which he had already built. He considered it would be a beautiful conclusion to his work if in his lifetime he could see the church which he had undertaken to reconstruct for the remission of his sins and in compensation for his vow brought to completion with the pontifical blessing.

There approached that day, happier than other feasts, when Jesus our Saviour took on this mortal coil and came forth from the Virgin's womb like a bridegroom from his chamber: on that day all the peerage of England were to gather at court, and witness the king resplendent as usual with sceptre and crown. Pondering therefore how he might enhance the solemnity of the consecration, he decreed that after the royal ceremonial was over, the celebration should take place on Holy Innocents' Day.

On the very night of the Lord's Nativity he was taken with a fever, and at once the merrymaking was turned to grief, the feastday to mourning. He covered this up, inspired, as I believe, by two consoling thoughts: firstly that he knew his passing to eternity to be not far distant, and secondly that it was the holy festival of the joyful birth of the joyous Jesus: a feast that brought him much gladness of heart.

For three days therefore he triumphed over nature and repressed his own sickness while wearing the regalia, and joined at table with the bishops and nobles with all the joviality he could muster. On the third day, knowing his time of summons to be near, he asked for everything to be made ready to consecrate the church on the following day. He prepared his own contribution, set out various ornaments, sorted out the different kinds of vessel, and made an inventory of all the property which was to go to endow, to adorn and to enrich that sacred monastery.

The day of the Holy Innocents dawned, and the bishops gathered, together with all the peers of the realm, to begin the holy rites of consecration. The king took part in the ceremony as far as his illness would allow him, but the queen arranged everything, provided everything, took care of and oversaw everything, to fulfil the duties of them both.

When everything this great ceremony required had been done the king laid his head back on his couch as if to say "It is consummated". From then on he was racked by great pain; everyone was griefstricken, and there was a general common lamentation. Most of them foresaw that his death would bring ruin to the nation, desolation for the people, the slaughter of all the nobility of England, the end of their freedom and the extinction of their honour.

The Consecration of Westminster Abbey. (Westminster Abbey.)

# 26: Of the Vision which he saw at the last

The courtiers stood around, while the queen crouched over his bed, warming his frozen limbs with her own bosom. Here he was, either sunk in sleep, or crushed by the nature of his illness, or (as one might believe) rapt in mental ecstasy, lying motionless for two days. At last, as if waking from a deep sleep, he opened his eyes and sat up, raising his hands towards heaven, and spoke:

"Almighty God, in whose hand all things do rest, you know all things before they be, you change kingdoms and transfer powers, and visit the wickedness of fathers on their sons; if what I have witnessed comes from the true light, grant me strength of voice, clear speech sounding well in my mouth, that I may recount your marvels, and those who hear me may learn to revere you, and with a humble spirit and contrite heart be pleasing in your presence. Grant too that you may relent from the woe which you have intended for this people."

Amazing! He had hardly ended his prayer when strength returned to his body and power to his voice: grace untied the strings which sickness had set on his tongue. The witnesses were astounded at how he, who a moment before had been so crushed by disease that they could hardly hear him, should suddenly raise his voice and speak with his old vigour and clarity of speech restored. The holy man, using the form of a parable, recounted this vision in clarion tones:

"When I was a lad in Normandy, I was always delighted to have good friends, and I was especially intimate with whomsoever seemed the best in the holy monasteries, those sheepfolds of religion. Among these men two in particular were tied to me with a special love, for their respectable way of life, their holy profession, their gentle manners and friendly speech. I visited them often, and their conversation was more delightful to my senses than a mouthful of honeycomb. That was my way of life then, and my inspiration was from such as they.

"Many years ago those two passed on to heaven, but I saw them a while ago attending my dreams, recounting to me what God had decreed would happen to my people after my death. They said England's wickedness had come to its fullness, and that evil once come to fruition was provoking tribulation and bringing on the judgement. 'Priests have broken their covenant with the Lord, and offer the sacrifice with corrupt hearts and guilty hands: not shepherds but hirelings, exposing the flock to wolves, not guarding it; seeking the milk and wool but not the sheep, till death feeds alike on shepherds and sheep, thrust down to Hell.

"'The earthly rulers too are faithless, fellows of thieves and looters of their country: with neither fear of God nor respect for men, they make a burden of truth, scorn justice and delight in cruelty. Thus neither do the rulers preserve justice nor the subjects discipline. See, the Lord rattles his sword, strings his bow and makes it ready! Henceforth he will show his people wrath and indignation, sending against them angels of punishment, in whose power they will be for a year and a day to be chastised by fire and the sword alike.'

"Thus they spoke, but I was griefstricken at the disaster that threatened my nation. 'What if they knew of heaven's secret design,' I said, 'and repented, and did penance? Would not God forgive them and leave a blessing behind him? Surely it was penance that held off the sentence pronounced by God against Nineveh, and deferred the merited death that hung over the wicked Ahab. Let me persuade my people to do penance for the past and be careful over the future: thus God may have mercy on them and not bring this great evil upon them. Those whom he prepared to punish as enemies, let him receive as converts, graced with his accustomed love.'

"'It cannot be', they said, 'for this people's heart is grown hard, their eyes are bleared and their ears heavy: they can neither hear reproof, nor understand rebuke, nor respect warnings nor be stirred by past benefits.'

"I grew even more concerned at these words, and enquired,

'Shall God therefore be angry for ever? Can he not ordain things so that he can be more kindly hereafter? When shall joy succeed to such sadness? What recompense can console after so many disasters? What remedy can be hoped for in these ills, so that the affliction which frightens and saddens us now may be balanced by a promise of even a little divine mercy?'

"To this the saintly men responded with this oracle: 'A certain green tree was cut from its stump and removed three furlongs from its own roots; when it returns to its stump, with no hand of man to urge, or necessity to drive, and sets itself on its ancient root, when the sap flows again, and it blossoms once more and produces fruit, then there will be some hope of comfort in this sorrow, and a remedy for the disaster we have predicted.' And when they had said this, they returned to heaven, and I to you."

While he was telling his vision, the queen sat by him, and also Robert, guardian of the sacred palace, Earl Harold, the queen's brother, and Stigand who had invaded his father's chamber and defiled his bed (for while Archbishop Robert was still alive, he usurped the see of Canterbury - suspended for this by the Supreme Pontiff, a little later he burst open and his bowels all poured out). He was hardened when he heard the king's story, and was neither afraid of the revelation nor believed in the prophecy, but instead, muttering that the king was senile and raving, he preferred laughter to compunction.

The others however, who were more sensible, wept copiously and sighed, for they were well aware that priests and nobles alike behaved precisely as the king had said. They remembered that such reports had often been made to the Supreme Pontiff, and that he in turn had frequently rebuked this decadence both by envoys and letters; the king and queen had taken steps to reform these abuses, but to no avail.

They discovered eventually that these prophecies were no mere imagination of the saintly king when Earl Harold seized the kingdom, breaking the oath which he had made to Duke William. When he was conquered by him in battle he brought the freedom of England to an end and began her captivity. Then some declared that what the King had prophesied in the foretold parable was impossible; those in particular who deplored the deaths of the entire nobility of England, for of that race there hardly remained any to be seen in England, neither King nor bishop nor abbot nor lord.

# 27: An Explanation of the Riddle set by the King

I think very differently, remembering that Saint Dunstan also predicted this calamity, and promised better times as well. It will not be inapposite to explain this here. The tree symbolises the Kingdom of England, resplendent in glory, fertile with wealth and delights, honourable in the dignity of its royalty. The root from which all this honour derives was the royal blood, which descends in a true line of succession from Alfred, the first of the English, they say, to be anointed and consecrated as king by the Supreme Pontiff, down to Saint Edward.

The tree was "cut from its stump" when the kingdom was taken from the royal family and given to another stock; it was "removed three furlongs from its own roots" when during the time of three kings there was no mixture of the new and the ancient royal lines. For Harold succeeded Edward, and William Harold, and William the second his father William. The tree "returns to its stump" when the glorious King Henry, in whom was concentrated the whole honour of the Kingdom, took for his wife Matilda, the great-niece of Edward, neither driven by necessity nor urged by the hope of gain, but out of pure love for her. Thus he joined the English and Norman lines, and by the consummation of his marriage made the two one.

The tree "blossomed" when the Empress Matilda was born from the two lines, and it "bore fruit" when from her arose our own Henry, like the morning star, like the corner stone joining together the two nations. Now indeed England has a king of English race; of the same stock she has bishops and abbots, barons as well, and perfect knights who, begotten by the mingling of both races, give honour to one and consolation to the other.

If this explanation does not please you, suggest another

yourself, or wait until another age to see these things unfold: let not one prophet be found contradicting another, let us not believe that Saint Edward could deny what we know Saint Dunstan promised! So having inserted this, not irrelevantly I trust, let us return to the course of our narrative.

# 28: Of the Death and Burial of the Holy King

The king was well aware that the hour was near for him to pass from this world to Christ. He urged his friends to spare their tears, and not to disturb by their futile lamentations the joy brought him by his hope. He rallied the bystanders, as it were, with these words:

"If you loved me, you would be glad that I am going to the Father, that I am to receive the joys promised to the faithful - not that I deserve them, but the Lord our Saviour in his grace has mercy on whom he wishes and offers his salvation to those he pleases. Your part is to accompany your friend with prayers, and by your psalms and almsgiving frustrate those demons who are obstructing my way to Heaven, for although my faith in the Crucified One cannot be overcome by such opponents, nevertheless hardly anyone is so perfect that they are unable to impede him or frighten him."

He then entrusted the queen to her brother and the nobility, and commended her devoted service. He proclaimed her modesty, for she played the part of a wife in public, but in private she was to him as a sister or daughter. He gave order as well that all the regal wealth she had conferred on him by way of a dowry, should be her free and unimpeded property for ever.

Those also who had followed him from Normandy he earnestly commended to the natives, whether they chose to return to their own country with thanks, or to remain here with honour. He requested that he should be buried in the church of the Blessed Apostle Peter which he had virtually rebuilt, and that his death should be speedily announced to all, lest any delay in notifying his death should hinder the help of prayer.

With everything properly in order, the saint asked the priests and ministers of the church to approach, and he shortly fortified himself for departure by receiving the Body and Blood of the Lord. When he saw that the queen was weeping more copiously than the others and sighing more deeply, he said, "Do not cry, my daughter: I am not to die but to live, and withdrawing from this land of the dead, I trust I shall see the Lord's goodness in the land of the living."

At last, entrusting himself totally to God, he departed this life in the faith of Christ, under Christ's sacraments, relying on the promises of Christ: an old man and full of days. His pure spirit left his virginal body and was wedded to the Creator of Spirits in eternal life. The citizens of heaven came to meet him; the keybearer of the sky opened heaven; John, the disciple whom Jesus loved, ran to meet him, true to the fulfilment of his promise; and with that virgin, our virgin follows the Lamb wherever he goes!

He died in the year of the Lord's Incarnation 1066 when he had reigned twenty three years, six months and twenty seven days; in the Fourth Indiction, the day before the Nones of January. With him fell virtually all the happiness of England; liberty perished, all power was lost. I cannot tell how great a fear soon fell on everyone, what sorrow overwhelmed them, what a dark despair filled the whole island.

The king's relations and friends stood around his deathbed, when suddenly the body offered glowing evidence of his future bliss, for a heavenly light shone on his face, and drew the eyes of all who were present. Amazed, they stripped the body, and its glory increased their amazement, for it shone with such a pure light that the splendour of his virginity could not escape even the most incredulous. They prepared straightway the royal funeral, wrapped the body in precious cloth and the best winding sheet, and the poor of Christ were cheered by generous almsgiving.

Bishops arrived, priests and a great concourse of clergy; the leaders of the kingdom, earls and other nobles collected, and battalions of monks congregated. An immense crowd of both sexes gathered from villages and towns for the king's funeral.

Psalms resounded on this side; tears and groans echoed from that. Joy was everywhere obscured by grief, for all saw in the king a cause for gladness, and one for sorrow in themselves.

They brought him to the church, that temple of purity, that abode of virtue: for him they offered the sacrifice of salvation. Thus he was laid to rest with honour in the place which he had chosen for himself; at the day of doom he will be gifted with the glorious resurrection through Jesus Christ our Lord, to whom be honour and glory for ever and ever. Amen!

# The Life of Saint Edward, Book Two

## 29: Of the Hunchback cured at his tomb

Once freed from human cares, Saint Edward could not conceal from the world how influential he was in heaven, nor could the virtue of his virginal remains be covered with earth or sealed with a stone, still less buried with his body. Indeed the power which remained in his limbs erupted into miracles, and as he restored sight to the blind, walking to the lame and health to the sick, our Edward made it clear and free from doubt that his death was "precious in the eyes of the Lord".

Among the poor men that the saint had helped while he was alive was a man named Ralph, a Norman by race. His thigh sinues had contracted so that his feet were doubled back to his buttocks, and he was not able to walk normally, and not even capable of crawling on his knees as most do who are afflicted like that, because of the pain. Mother Necessity had found him a novel form of aid, for he acquired a hollow vessel, shaped like a bowl, and settled his behind and the contracted limbs in it, so that crouching closely, he could support his front with his hands, and drag his posterior as if sailing on dry land.

The king had passed above, and the wretch was missing his accustomed alms, finding it even more difficult to sustain his disability. But he remembered the Man of God who had fed him when he was alive, whose holiness could hardly escape his notice and admiration, and full of confidence he made his way in his cockleshell to the tomb of the holy king within a week of his burial. There he spoke to the king as if alive:

"Are you not the one who used to cure the weak and ill by heavenly power while you were still walking about in a mortal body? Now, my Lord, while you were alive I could bear my crippled limbs a little easier, since they were the reason why I

96

received abundance of food, drink, entertainment and necessary clothing. But now poverty piles upon my infirmity, and you will either have to tell me what to do, where to go, whose majesty to apply to, whose piety to invoke, or you yourself will have to offer a healing hand as you used to, for although it would be unlawful for me to aspire to the spiritual delights you now enjoy, yet you have the power to restore my limbs, with which I can enjoy bodily ones."

He had hardly finished speaking when the king's holiness flashed out, his grace blossomed, the piety which had been challenged shone forth. An unseen power suddenly stretched his sinues to their proper length, straightened his legs and feet, and as his joints emerged from their embedding flesh the blood flowed again, his vigour was gradually renewed, and the bones which had been dried up regained their original strength. The bystanders rejoiced that the same power was evident in the dead man that they had seen while he was alive, and from then on people began to visit the relics of Saint Edward more frequently and honour them more carefully, knowing that an apostolic grace would not be far from them for the curing of the sick and dispersing of disease.

The man concerned stood on his own feet, giving thanks to God and Saint Edward, whose first grace had been to feed his weakened body, and who had added the second grace of removing the infirmity altogether.

# 30: Of Six Blind Men and a One-Eyed Man given sight at his tomb

I have described how Saint Edward had a special power to enlighten the blind while he was yet alive, and the following chapter will show that the accident of death had not deprived him of it. They were celebrating the third anniversary of the king's death when six blind men led by a one-eyed man clustered round the royal tomb. It was a remarkable sight to see one led by the other, and a single eye in front providing guidance to seven. The one who directed the steps of all arranged them before the shrine of the holy body, and they set forth their woes in tears, begged for help, and besought the blessed king's help against the weariness of eternal darkness.

They did not consider it difficult for the Lord of Light to grant their request for light to their mortal bodies, since he dwells in the realm of light where night never intrudes. Nor did they think that Edward would be of less repute among the choirs of angels than he had been while yet wrapped in his corruptible flesh. Since they persevered in their prayers, the help of God did not fail them, so that he might more widely declare the merits of his saint, as well as granting the solace the wretches desired. For all at once he who had been the leader of the others received the reward of his charity with the redoubling of his eyesight, and looking back at his companions, saw that they too were exulting in the gift of new light.

They looked at each other, and each inquired whether the other could see; all were amazed, and as if beside themselves, unsure whether what had happened was true, they thought they were seeing a vision. At length they came to themselves, and recognised the great abundance of divine mercy, breaking into cries of joy and gratitude; many others ran up and were stupefied with joy, praising God in Edward, his saint. Those who had received the healing grace gave thanks to God and returned to their homes, proclaiming the merits of the blessed king, and proving his virtue with the evidence of their restored sight.

# 31: Of the Victory which the Holy King merited for King Harold

Harold meanwhile, the son of Godwine, had impiously usurped the kingdom, although he had promised on oath that he would preserve it for William, the cousin-german of King Edward. He had neither legal nor natural right to this, and by breaking faith and ignoring his promise he hastened on the woes which the king had prophesied the Lord was preparing for England.

In order that his strength might be lessened and he be more easily vanquished by the foes he had unjustly provoked, God raised up another enemy for him from the North, Harold, known as Hardrada, King of Norway, and Tostig, the brother whom he had himself driven from England and exiled to Flanders in King Edward's time. These two came up the Humber to York with a great fleet, engaged the Northumbrian army in battle, and on obtaining the victory made a great slaughter among those who resisted.

This was relayed to Harold, and he gathered a vast army from all parts of England. Then one night Saint Edward appeared in a dream to a certain holy abbot, who governed the monastery of Ramsey, Alsinus by name. The man was wise enough to be overawed by his majesty, but the king mildly reassured him: "Go," he said, "and tell Harold that he may confidently attack these men who have invaded the territory of this kingdom against all legal right. I myself shall be leader and guardian of the army, for I cannot in justice desert my people, through whose help he will return in triumph over this enemy.

"And lest he disbelieve your words, reveal to him this secret of his own heart, so that when you uncover his thoughts, of which none were aware, he will ascribe this message not to your imagination but to my authority. For last night he was racked with pain, and although the illness that hung over him was not light he kept quiet about it, considering that if he announced his illness he would earn the contempt of his own men and the derision of his enemies. Tell him this, so that now his weakness has given place to strength, and he has recovered from the disease, he may rely on my help and wage a just war against the barbarians to deliver his people from the danger that threatens."

The reverend abbot woke from sleep and came to Harold, delivered him the prophecy, and lest he hesitate in doubt, revealed to his great amazement the secret which the saint had bade him tell. Harold then, encouraged by this promise from heaven, advanced with a strong hand as far as Yorkshire and engaged the enemy in the place then called Stamford Bridge, but now known as Battlebridge from that event. In the heat of battle both their leaders fell, the King, that is, of Norway, and Tostig, own brother to the King of England, and virtually all their army were destroyed. So it was that what the saint had long before prophesied about the two brothers when they were still boys, and foretold in a recent vision, was brought to pass by Harold's one victory, as nobody can deny.

# 32: How a blind man saw Saint Edward rise from his tomb and so received his sight

There was a young man of respectable birth in the monastery of the Blessed Apostle Peter, good looking, but deprived of the use of both eyes. The superiors of the monastery at that time were sorry for his misfortune, and set him to ring the bells which informed the brothers when they were to set to work, and to indicate with the clash of cymbals the hours appointed for the different services. The man carried out the office entrusted to him with diligence, he was regularly in the church, followed the prayers assiduously, and constantly prayed for the help of the saintly king.

It happened one day in summer, when the brothers were taking their midday rest, that he lay down in the chapel to ease his limbs - and lo, he saw Saint Edward, in a dream, rising from his tomb and looking at him. Then chiding the man for his drowsiness, he bade him ring the bell to end the rest and summon the brethren to the hour of None, which was almost overdue. When the saint had given him this order, he saw the king advance, crowned, towards the altar. Watching him carefully, he fixed his eyes on the flashing splendour of his halo, till the holy vision disappeared.

The young man, dazed, opened his eyes suddenly, and at the inrush of light realised that he had regained his former sight. He revealed the vision to the brothers, and the evidence of the miracle confirmed his words. All wondered, and blessed God for his works, for he had granted blessed Edward a fuller life after his death, and made his dead bones flourish in miracles from the grave.

# 33: Of the unjust deposition of Saint Wulfstan and of his lawful restoration by the saintly King

The Lord is gracious to those who fear him, and his mercy is on those who hope in him. This was proved by the simple goodness of Saint Wulfstan, and the magnificent power of Saint Edward, in the following miracle.

When King William had subdued the whole island, and all who resisted him had been either driven overseas, secured in prison or bound in slavery, he began to meddle in church affairs with his henchmen. He had a synod called in the presence of the legates of the Holy See, Ermenfrid, Bishop of Sion, and the Cardinal priests John and Peter. By these Stigand (whom as we have mentioned was defiling God's sanctuary with his polluted feet) was stripped of his rank and dignity, and the king condemned him to perpetual imprisonment. Abbot Lanfranc succeeded him in the see of Canterbury, a man learned in many fields, expert in all the liberal arts as well as theology and literature. He was as it were commissioned by God to root out, to tear down and to destroy, to build and to plant, attempting to restore the English Church to renewed beauty, relying on his legatine authority. He set to work at once to correct abuses and to make necessary decrees, urging both priests and monks to live more religious lives.

Wulfstan, a man of God, was accused before Lanfranc of being too simple and inexperienced, a man ignorant and unlearned, who ought to be deposed. This was decreed, with the King's consent, or rather at his express command. Accordingly at the synod which was held at Westminster under Lanfranc, in the King's presence, among the other affairs dealt with there, he bade the reverend man surrender his staff and ring. The man of God was disturbed neither in mind nor countenance, but stood up and held out his pastoral staff:

"Truly, my Lord Archbishop," he said, "I know well that I am not worthy of this honour, nor suitable to this charge nor equal to this task: I was aware of this when the clergy elected me, the bishops persuaded me and my Lord King Edward summoned me to this position. It was he, with the authority of the Holy See, who laid this burden on my shoulders, and with this Staff invested me to assume the rank of bishop. And now you request my pastoral staff, which you never gave me; you take away the office which you never conferred on me. I indeed am not unconscious of my unworthiness, and I will resign my staff in obedience to the decree of this holy synod, but not to you - rather to him by whose authority I received it."

He said this, and then proceeded with his followers to the stone which covered the remains of the glorious king. Standing before the grave he said:

"You know, my Lord Edward, how unwillingly I undertook this burden, how often I tried to escape from it, how often I was missing when they sought for me. I admit that I am foolish, but you persuaded me to it. Now, albeit the brothers elected me, the people asked for me, the bishops consented and the nobles approved, it was above all your authority that settled the matter, your desire that prevailed over me.

"But see now, a new king, a new constitution, a new primate: they make new laws and promulgate new decisions. They convict you of error in commanding me, me of presumption in consenting. Perhaps indeed you could have been wrong then like any man, but surely not now you are close to God? It is not for them who demand what they did not grant, who are like all men liable to deceive and to be deceived, but for you who granted, you who are now in the presence of truth itself and free from all darkness of error and ignorance, to you, I say, shall I surrender the staff, to you I resign the care of those you commended to me, to you I entrust them with confidence, for I know well your capability."

So saying, he lifted his hand somewhat, and plunged his staff into the stone which covered the holy relics. "Take it, my Lord

King," he said, "and grant it to whomsoever you will." And so he came down from the altar, put off his episcopal robes and sat down among the monks as a simple monk himself.

All were astounded to see the staff fixed into the stone, and as if firmly rooted leaning neither to left nor right. Some made an attempt to pull it out, but it stood fast. There arose a grumbling murmur among the crowd, and sightseers came from all sides to witness the power of God. They hesitated, came a little closer, stopped still again, held a hand out, drew it back, dropped on the floor to examine how the metal entered the stone, stood up again to encourage each other to come and see.

The affair was referred back to the Synod. Lanfranc refused to believe what he was told, and summoned Gundulf, Bishop of Rochester, a reverend and pious man, and ordered him to go to the tomb and bring back the staff which the saint had left there. The lesser bishop obeyed his superior, but the strength of the virginal body, dead though it were, was greater than the living bishop's hand. He attempted to pull the staff out, but the saint, lying below him indeed but above him in power, held onto the lower part of it with an amazing force, so that it remained stuck fast in the rock.

Then Archbishop Lanfranc was astounded at this novel miracle, and wishing the king to witness this marvel, sent for him to come to the synod. Lanfranc rose to greet him as he and his retinue arrived, and they went together to the royal tomb. The archbishop prayed, stretched out his hand and attempted to tug out the staff, but the royal saint was obstinate and his efforts failed in their desired effect. The king cried out, the archbishop wept, and both acclaimed God's glory and Edward's praise, for he had declared by unmistakable signs that he had made no mistake in promoting Wulfstan.

Lanfranc then addressed the saint: "Truly the Lord is just and loves justice, his face looks on equity, truly he walks with the simple and his conversation is with the lowly minded. My brother, we were scornful of your holy simplicity, but your righteousness has been made to shine like a light, and your cause like the noonday sun. We must deplore the darkness which made us call evil good and good evil. Our judgement of you, brother, has been erroneous indeed, and God has raised up the spirit of his king to quash our sentence and proclaim to all that your simplicity is pleasing to God.

"Therefore, with the authority entrusted to us, nay by the divine judgement which has vanquished us, we return to you the cure which we ill-advisedly stripped from you, and we lay it on you knowing by experience that for a just man a little suffices for more than the great riches of sinners. Better indeed is a little learning with faith which works in simplicity and love, rather than the wealth of wisdom and worldly learning which so many misuse either for the empty praise of men or the pursuit of base gain. Come near, therefore, my brother, come to your master, who is ours as well, for we believe that his holy hand which has kept the staff from us will gladly open and resign it to you."

When he heard this, the saintly bishop did as he was told, in his usual simple manner, and went up to the altar. "See," he said, "My Lord Edward, see how I am entrusted to your judgement, as I have surrendered myself to your decision in resigning to you the staff you gave me. What now is your pleasure, what do you desire, what do you decree? Indeed you have preserved your dignity, vindicated my innocence and made your greatness known. Accordingly if your original opinion of me remains yet, return the staff to me, or if it has changed, reveal to whom it should be passed."

So saying, he tugged lightly at the staff, which came away in his hand and rose as if it had been stuck into soft mud. The king and the archbishop came up at once to beg his pardon on their knees, and they commended themselves to the holy man's prayers. He however, who had learned from the Lord to be lowly and humble of heart, knelt in turn before them and asked the blessing of so great an archbishop.

Who could recount what tears there were among the holy

106

bishops, what sighs, what humble rivalry in seeking his blessing? At last with mutual blessings and clasping of hands they all returned gladly to the synod; many were in tears for very joy, all proclaimed that God does wonderful things for his saints. The king moreover, fired with love for his cousin and predecessor, had a feretory wrought with gold and silver for his holy shrine, as you may still see today, adorned with marvellous skill.

St. Wulfstan inserts his crosier in St. Edward's tomb
(Engraving from Porter.)

# 34: Of his first translation, and the Incorruption of his Body

Since Saint Edward had blossomed forth in such great miracles, there was frequent discussion of his holiness among the monks. Day by day their devotion for their great patron grew, and they became more and more eager to examine his holy relics. There arose among them a general but friendly argument, for some asserted that the virginal flesh of the king would be innocent of corruption, and remain whole and perfect in the holy reliquary about his body, while others were more cautious, and urged the former to keep silent about their presumption, lest their hope be proved vain and the glory of such a great confessor be needlessly diminished.

"For since," they said, "the bodies of the apostles, the martyrs and innumerable saints have been reduced to dust, if the natural course has applied to Edward, he should be no less beloved by us, nor seem any less acceptable to God."

While this dispute was being aired in front of the reverend man Gilbert Crispin, who was abbot of that monastery, they decided in any event to investigate their great patron's body, and determine for certain which opinion was correct. He appointed a day therefore to bring the holy man's relics into the open, to resolve the faith of some, the fears of others. To this heavenly display he invited respectable and pious people, among whom was Gundulf, Bishop of Rochester, whom we have already mentioned, and who outshone the others in grace and dignity.

Accordingly, thirty six years after he departed this human life, those who were invited came to the holy man's tomb, and removed the slab which covered the coffin. Such a fragrant odour assailed their nostrils, that the church was full of it, and they imagined the coffin to be filled with spices. They observed that the first shroud which wrapped the sacred limbs had preserved its original beauty and strength. Encouraged with the hope of greater wonders, they removed the shroud and examined the other ornaments and clothes, finding all firm and whole.

They lifted his arms, flexed his fingers, felt his joints, and found all to be whole, flexible and firm with their original consistancy. Eventually they examined the integrity and colour of his flesh, which was as pure as glass, as white as snow, and prefigured the glory of his coming resurrection. All were eager to touch his beloved face, but were at the same time afraid, till the Bishop of Rochester, more confident because of his love and clear conscience, laid his hand on the veil which covered his sacred head. Lifting the lower part, he was bold enough to pull at the beard, which was snowy white, and felt that it was attached to his chin as firmly as if he were still alive.

Delighted at the miracle, and moved with longing, he attempted to remove a single hair as a keepsake, but it held firm, and his wish came to nothing. Gilbert noticed this, and mildly rebuked the bishop. "Leave it, Father," he said, "do not disturb this great king's repose, nor diminish the integrity which Christ has preserved so long."

"You are right, my lord abbot," the bishop replied, "but do not attribute my attempt to presumption but rather devotion, for I should be wealthier than Crœsus if I could be enriched with even a tiny portion of his relics. But since the royal will disdains anything to be removed from him, let him keep all, and await the day of his joyous resurrection whole and complete."

Accordingly they retained the shroud with which his sacred limbs had been wrapped, and replaced it with another of equal value, and carefully returned that precious clay into its resting place. There many more miracles take place through his merits, and I shall recount just a few out of so many, for the praise of Our Lord Jesus Christ.

# 35: Of a Girl, cured at his Tomb

The holy prophet Elisha was mocked by more than forty little boys, and avenging his wrong with a curse, abandoned the whole lot to be punished by bears. Saint Peter condemned the wicked magician Elymas to sudden blindness, because he had blasphemed the apostles. Christ himself declares that an injury to one of his saints redounds onto himself, for he said "He who hears you hears me, and he who rejects you rejects me." This too the Lord Jesus shows to his Edward, punishing with great strictness those who detract from his sanctity, and rewarding with many benefits those who revere him.

There was in the city a noblewoman, Matilda by name, very skilled in embroidery. She used to enhance the robes of royalty and the rich with gold, stud them with jewels and adorn them in needlework with scenes and flowers. She was commissioned for some expensive work by a certain noble lady, who was very rich, and being engaged to the Earl of Gloucester, ranked not far below the queen. She was determined to excel the other countesses of England in the splendour of her wardrobe, as she already did in her wealth. She came daily to insist that everything should be got ready not only with the greatest skill but with haste as well.

There arrived the principal feast of Saint Edward, King and Martyr, the uncle of our sovereign: he was the one who was blameless but slain by the wicked, and is believed to have been crowned with the martyrdom of innocence. The sagacious woman was undecided: she knew that she would incur the wrath of the haughty lady for delaying the task, but feared she would be liable to divine vengeance for violating the sacred festival with prohibited work. She turned therefore to her associate, a young woman:

"What do you decide betwen the urgency of this work and the festival of the holy King Edward? It seems to me that to be idle would be profitless, but to work would be dangerous on

110

such a solemnity."

The girl laughed: "Is that the Edward which the common herd venerate as a king at Westminster? What have I to do with him? Let others be idle and mourn the dead with their singing, or honour him indeed: I'm not going to abandon the work I have begun, not for him, no more than for a peasant, even if you do tell me to!"

The mistress was afraid and grew indignant: thinking it over, her wrath eventually burst out with loud and shocked rebuke: she castigated the blasphemer as if she had been possessed by the devil, with severe reproaches. But the apprentice sneered, mocking her mistress' foolishness. She piled mockery on mockery, till suddenly, in front of many, she was seized by a paralytic stroke: her blaspheming mouth was twisted up to her right ear, and she was deprived of the use of the tongue she had misused. Her lips writhed, she gnashed her teeth and they grew dry; her whole body went into painful convulsions.

When the girl's mistress saw that this had come about by the just judgment of God, her wrath gave way to grief, her anger to tears. She wept, and her whole household with her. The one that she had reviled as a blasphemer she now pitied for suffering so much intolerable pain. The matter was noised in the city, and many came to console the mistress or to gape at the apprentice.

While she was debating what to do, a personage of considerable dignity appeared, and instructed her to place the poor girl on a boat, and take her to the holy relics that she had blasphemed, and that she would receive relief by the merits of him whom she had offended and so suffered such a dire punishment.

It was done as he said: the unfortunate woman was taken to the saintly king's tomb, a candle was lit as long as herself, and her mistress was diligent in prayer and vigil. There was a great lamentation around her, for the terrible illness she suffered seemed incurable. The only hope they all had was in the piety of Edward, who had learnt from the Lord Jesus to repay evil with good, hatred with love.

She remained in pain all that night, while the others wept and prayed. The brothers of the monastery prayed for her as well, and their superior conducted a solemn litany for her with great devotion. In the sight of the holy king competed prayer and sickness, the wickedness of the sinful servant and the faith of her merciful mistress, the greatness of the crime and the amount of her grief.

At length that pardon which so often prevails, through the merits of the saintly king prevailed over Jesus: soon mild mercy moderated the sentence which justice had decreed, overruling right in the case of the sick girl. And so it was that she continued in pain for a night and a day, but at the hour when the sacred duties of that day were being concluded with vespers, suddenly she found herself restored to wholeness, among the chanting voices and sobbing prayers.

She gazed at the company, puzzled by their tears: her speech returned and she asked where she was, what had happened, how had she come there, and what was the reason for such grief. Her mouth, which the disease had twisted, had returned to its proper form: she recovered her former beauty along with her sanity. When she heard all that had happened she burst into tears: her mouth, tongue, mind and intelligence proclaimed her repentance, and heavy sighs betrayed her inner contrition.

Then those who stood by sang of the mercy and justice of the Lord, who strikes and also heals, he gives death and also life, he leads down to hell and brings up again. The girl, giving thanks to God and his holy servant Edward, returned unharmed home with her mistress. From then on, whenever she heard the name of the glorious king, she was so shaken by fear that her face would go pale and shuddering overtake her whole body.

# 36: Of a certain Monk freed by the saintly King from a Quartan Fever

There was a brother named Osbert in the monastery where Saint Edward's holy relics were preserved: his exemplary way of life was adorned with knowledge, enlivened with eloquence and greatly enriched with science both natural and theological. One day about the middle of July he was seized by a quartan fever, and troubled with it for about six months, for it seems to be the nature of the disease to be recurrent. His flesh was wasted, his blood weakened, his bones empty of marrow made him seem more ghost than man.

There arrived the feast of the Lord's birth, which all people celebrate, and our man was oppressed by a double grief; not only was he racked by the force of his disease, but he considered it more grievious still that he could not attend the joyous celebrations. Faith therefore brought strength to nature, and devotion triumphed over disease: against all expectation the man of God was brought to join in the sacred vigils.

And now about cockcrow the Mass was celebrated, as is the custom of the Church on that day. The gospel was being chanted where Saint Luke the evangelist describes the virginal birth, the shepherds' watch, the angels' attendance. The sick monk was wrapt in loving contemplation of the lowliness of the child born for us, and the love of the virgin mother; dissolving totally into tears, he was amazingly filled with inner joy, and his withered limbs were replenished with outward fairness.

He sang psalms, with mind and spirit alike; both mind and spirit joined in prayer: between Mother and Son, between womb and manger, flitted his reverent thought and speech. He came to believe that the illness he had suffered so long was over: but sweet Jesus had only suspended, not extinguished it, so that he might advance the merits of his Edward. For two days the man's fever was restrained by some divine power for the sake of his devotion, but on the third day it attacked his poor body with greater severity than before, and invading his limbs, sinues and joints, nay his innards too, dried up his whole being with pains and agonies both inward and external.

Among these torments, when each day seemed more dreadful than the last, there arrived the day he longed for, when the glorious sovereign Edward at the end of his earthly renown merited his heavenly reward from Christ. Therefore at the time when the saving sacrifice was being offered in memory of the great king, he came feebly to the holy shrine and lay on the ground, grieving as if he were about to surrender his soul.

My God, what groans, what sighs, what sobs shook that wretched body! What words did pain dictate to him, did faith suggest, did hope compound! Now he called out as if persuading, now he begged as if beseeching. "How long, O Lord, how long? Will you forget me for ever? Will you turn your face ever away from me? Where are now, I beg, your marvels of which our fathers have told us, the works which you did in their days? Will not you, who are accustomed to have mercy and to spare towards strangers, will you not open your heart of compassion to those who serve you, who are assigned to your praise, who are bound to your commands?

"Will you expose to be consumed by fever a body which you have so far nourished from the royal bounty? Not consumed swiftly, indeed, for alas I am devoured but not consumed, tormented but not to death, my life is pained, not ended, I long for death but it is not granted me. What shall I do, contending with you as with a judge, when I ask for mercy, can I not also rely on justice?

"I beg you therefore, good king, most loving sovereign, dear patron, may the great grief of your servant move your compassionate heart: look down with that eye which so often sees us from afar, see how I am affected in my pain-racked bowels, how unbearably I fluctuate from excessive heat to terrible cold! Oh horrible shivering, Oh unspeakable heat! Listen, most gracious Lord, listen and see if there is any sorrow like unto my sorrow! If you deem me unworthy of health, at least end my pain in death."

His words were interrupted by sobs and tears, he pleaded his case no more by words but in gesture. At last, when the Mass was over, he rose from prayer - and lo, all his pain departed, and all his limbs recovered their original strength as if bathed by a fresh shower. He even began to think about food, and his nausea quickly departed, so that with eager appetite he longed for a meal.

What is there to add? Restored to perfect health he continued to be as devout in his service and praise of the holy confessor as the power he had felt in his own body warranted.

# 37: Of a certain Knight cured of the same Disease

This monk was a scribe who became a disciple of the kingdom of heaven, and whenever he was bidden preach to the people he brought out of his storechamber things both old and new. It happened that after he had recovered his health by this great miracle that a year passed and again brought the memorial anniversary of the saintly king's departure. No small crowd gathered from the city, as happened every year, and they joyfully took part not only in the Mass but in the office as well for his greater glory.

The monk, delegated by the abbot, put on his sacred vestments and came to the altar to celebrate Mass. After reading the holy Gospel, he turned to the people and preached to them on the king's holiness and virtue. The man of God hailed his humility, praised his patience, marvelled at his modesty. With tales of various miracles he proved how great his merits were in God's eyes. Finally he revealed how he himself had experienced his power the year before, and moved all to devotion, many indeed to sighs and tears.

There was present a knight, a guard at the royal palace, named Gerinus: he had been excessively troubled by a quartan fever for days and months, and had spent much in vain on doctors. For the disease spared neither him nor his property, emptying his purse of money, his body of blood. His soul was wearied, and he deemed nothing remained for him but the grave.

Hearing therefore that this monk had been freed from a similar disease through the merits of blessed Edward, hope followed on faith rekindled, and charity ignited his faltering heart. Filled with enthusiasm by all this, he kept vigil with lighted candles at the king's tomb the following night. It was the eve of the Epiphany of the Lord, and the night was celebrated with threefold joy, for the faith of the pagans, the sacrament of baptism and the beginning of Christ's miracles were commemorated.

In the monastery hymns echoed and readings droned on: Gerinus was totally intent on Edward, offering tears and multiplying prayers. Edward heard Gerinus, and Christ heard Edward: in a single action he rendered the king glorious and honourable, Gerinus sound, and the fever extinguished.

# 38: Of a Woman whom he Healed in her Absence

The ruler whose son was sick at Capharnaum thought that it was necessary for the Lord to be physically present to heal him: the Lord's own words rebuke his little faith. The centurion in contrast, we learn from Christ, had faith greater than any in Israel, because when the Lord proposed going himself to drive away the boy's paralysis, the centurion, fully confident in his divine majesty, said "No, Lord, but only say the word and my boy will be healed."

With confidence like that, a certain nun professed in the monastery of Barking, brought greater renown to the merits of blessed Edward by her own faith. For she also laboured under the burden of a quartan fever, and since already she was passing her second year under this disease, she had lost any hope of recovery. But one day when during the morning she was refreshing her wasted limbs with peaceful sleep, she saw in a dream herself with her companions making their way to visit her own home and her family. When they had gone a little way, one of them asked if they could turn off to Westminster, where they could be refreshed with food and drink for the easier continuance of their journey.

"How could I call on those monks," she replied, "since I have never met any of them, I don't know their names, nor have I ever had any communication or exchange of gifts with any of them?"

The first replied, "There lies the noble King Edward, and if you visit his tomb with devotion and faith, he will readily ask the Lord for you to receive healing which will restore your body to its wonted vigour."

The woman awoke, shaking off sleep, and rose from her bed; supporting her weak limbs with a stick, she entered the chapel and lay before the altar. She recited the seven psalms which are called the penitential ones with great contrition, and added the solemn Litany, then calling on the holy king with devout prayers, she said:

"I believe, my Lord, that healing is available for me at your holy tomb, as was promised to me, if I journey there: but what need is there for me to make this effort, incur indeed this danger? It would be no small interruption of my peace if I were to seek out a vehicle, acquire provision for the journey and choose companions. And what is more, the sights and sounds on the journey and return would excite my mind, diminish my recollection, and I myself might have to waste time in trifles, or wait on others doing so.

"What necessity is there for me to search out the presence of your holy body, when you are present in spirit? In the eyes of the Creator all creation is close together. I know indeed, I know for sure that in that light which perfuses all, my woes are open to you, and since you are a sharer in God's almighty power, if you wish it, you are not lacking in ability. Say but the word, and your handmaid shall be healed."

She cried out like this in great anguish of heart, and returned then to her bed, fearful and trembling, for it was the day on which she anticipated the recurrence of her attack of shivering. But the fever, proceeding so to speak with laggard step, brought little or no discomfort to the sufferer. The woman, encouraged by this, gave herself over completely to prayer to the saintly king, and after the respite of the two days awaited nervously the arrival of the quartan ague. When that fearful time arrived, she went again to the oratory, and having recited the psalms she wept again, and increased her prayers.

There is no more to add: she passed that day too without harm. When the third occasion of sickness had passed healed by the same antidote, she was restored to perfect health, and for as long as she lived she returned thanks to Saint Edward the King.

# 39: Of a Monk Cured from a Threefold Disease

I do not think I should pass over in silence what divine bounty has granted to another of the servants of Westminster, a religious and respectable man, through the merits of the blessed king. This man was remarkably devoted to Saint Edward: the repetition of his name and the memory of his holiness were sweeter to him than honey, than honey from the comb. As a sign of gratitude he used to recite five psalms every day for the repose of his soul.

It happened that he was afflicted with a triple grief, and no healing was to be hoped for save from heaven. For after bloodletting his blood gathered around the incision and clotted into a painful hard abcess. The pain spread to the surrounding area, and deprived him of the use of his arm. His heart also was constricted by his breathing, and his confined chest had great difficulty in emitting breath. Moreover an unbearable swelling in his foot made it almost impossible to use.

As the year came round the solemn day approached when the holy king had passed to the kingdom of heaven. The monk, labouring under such distress, awaited the celebration that all longed for with more sadness than usual. That night, at the appointed time when the whole crowd of brothers eagerly gathered to ring the bells in honour of the king, he sat sadly, hindered by his ill-health from showing any sign of rejoicing, or offering his brothers any cheer in their labours.

For as they pulled on the bellropes with great devotion, he was vexed, and unable to endure himself any longer cried out, "Why, O my Edward, do you not help me; why do you refuse me the strength to do what I wish? Come, I beg you, for I shall arise and join the choir of my brothers."

Disdaining his disease, he seized one of the ropes, and tugged with both hands with all his strength. The abcess burst at once, the rotten congealed blood gushed out and as the swelling subsided all pain disappeared. Relieved of one of his three diseases, he turned his concern to his chest, and having experienced the virtue of the holy king, he began to pray with bolder faith and more eager hope. For it was his custom, as the brothers returned to their beds after Vigils, to remain behind in the church and to give time to psalms and private prayer before one of the altars.

On the same night that he had felt the divine presence in the healing of his arm, he proceeded with reverence to the congenially quiet place he used to haunt. Prostrate before God and his holy Confessor Edward, he gave thanks for the benefit he had received, and begged for the one he had not. Nor should we think he showed presumption but rather faith when he prayed for the heavenly gift to be threefold. And so he persevered in tears and prayers, glad for his arm but grieving for his chest. While he was praying, a great sweat burst from his body, and this rendered his breathing as strong as ever. His chest, perfused with a dew from heaven, received its wonted health again.

There remained only the pain in his foot, which prevented him from joining the fellowship of his brothers. Therefore he slept in the infirmary with another elderly brother. One day about sunset they were regaling each other with conversation, and their talk turned to the happy recollection of the virtue of our saintly king. He who had already been cured from two diseases said:

"How great is the abundance of his power, dear brother, which I, a sinner, have experienced in myself! I am confident that whatever he wished he could easily obtain from the Lord God." He recounted the miracle that had happened to him, and stretched out his foot, deformed with its unbearable swelling. "If he were to remove my pain and cure this foot, I could not imagine anything further to ask of him."

They comforted each other with this conversation, and as the sun set took to their beds. But in the morning he whose foot was bad put his hand where the pain usually was, but found on his foot neither swelling nor pain: he realised he had been given complete health through the blessed Edward. He cried out for joy, and told his companions about the heavenly miracle: more fervent in his love, more devout in his praise, more forthright in setting forth the merits of his great patron, he stirred the hearts of all to the praise and glory of our Lord Jesus Christ, to whom be honour for ever and ever. Amen !

*Here ends the Life of Saint Edward*
*King and Confessor*
*and his miracles.*

# Appendix
## Extract from *Genealogia Regum Anglorum*

When Cnut and the sons who reigned after him were dead, there succeeded to the English throne Edward, the brother of Edmund, and son of Ethelred, who, as we have said, was exiled to Normandy. For his brother Alfred had died a cruel death in England, through the treachery as is thought of Godwine. And so when Edward came to England he was welcomed by the clergy and all the people with great rejoicing. On Easter day he was anointed and crowned king at Winchester by the Archbishops of Canterbury and York and almost all the episcopate of the realm. He walked in the ways of his ancestor Edgar: a mild and religious man, guarding his kingdom in peace, not by war. His temperament was such as to restrain anger, despise avarice and know nothing of pride.

Once he had established peace both at home and overseas, and made himself a friend and ally of the neighbouring kings and princes, he sent messages to the Roman Emperor asking that he would be so good as to send home his nephew, that is to say Edward, son of his brother Edmund Ironside, who was the rightful future heir to the kingdom. The emperor received the envoys graciously, and kept them some time with honour. At length, once ships had been made ready, and all that the travellers might require prepared, he sent forth Edward with his wife Agatha (the daughter of his cousin) and his children Edgar the Ætheling, Margaret and Christina. They came with great glory and riches, as the king had desired, and arrived in England after an easy voyage. Their coming brought joy to king and people alike, but the prince, dying a few days later, turned joy to grief, mirth to tears.

Not long after the king himself died: he was arranging the dedication with great solemnity of a noble monastery which he had founded in honour of St Peter on the west side of London, when he closed his praiseworthy life in a peaceful death, on the vigil of the Epiphany after a reign of twenty three years, six months and twenty seven days. The island was filled with tears and woe. When he had been buried as fitted such a one in the monastery I have mentioned, some attempted to elect as king Edgar the Ætheling, to whom the kingdom was due by right of heredity. But since the child was thought unsuitable for such an honour, in a tragic mistake Earl Harold obtained the kingdom, for he was more astute mentally, his purse was longer and his troops more numerous.

# Notes

## Prologue:

*Lawrence*, Abbot of Westminster, a kinsman of Aelred, reigned from 1160 to 1191, and was influential in securing the canonisation of Saint Edward, as well as the right for himself and his successors to wear the mitre.

*Henry II*, King of England 1154 to 1189, was the son of the Empress Matilda who was herself the daughter of Henry I, a Norman, and his wife Edith (or Matilda), a Saxon. Edith was the daughter of Malcolm Canmore, King of Scotland by his wife Margaret, great neice of St Edward. Henry II was thus the first to secure the throne of England by right both of the Saxon and Norman lines. King Malcolm's son David I adopted Aelred into the royal household, and had him brought up with his son and stepsons, so Henry II was the great-nephew of Aelred's childhood friend and patron (See Squire, p 12).

*Our Holy Mother the Church has decreed...* Edward was canonised by a Bull of Pope Alexander III written in Anagni in February 1161, two years before the writing of this Life.

*Prophetic parable* see chapters 26 and 27.

## Preface:

*Aelred* was Abbot of Rievaulx from 1147 to his death in 1167.

*In his days pleased God* is from the reading *Ecce Sacerdos Magnus*, a catena of texts from Ecclesiasticus used for confessor bishops.

*Begets virgins* Zechariah 9:27 (All scripture texts are from the Latin Vulgate).

*The original book* is Osbert's life which Lawrence had sent to Aelred. The letters are transcribed word for word from Osbert, but the interpretation of the prophecy (chapter 27) is more original to Aelred.

## Chapter 1:

*Saint Peter* Acts 10:34-5.

*Alfred* the Great was crowned King of Wessex by Pope Leo IV in 853.

*Ten hours' work* Aelred is a little muddled here: the reference is to the parable of the labourers (Matth. 20:1-16) but the full day was twelve hours, not ten.

*Edgar* is usually reckoned as the first king of all England, receiving the homage of eight lesser kings at Chester in 973.

*The forceful King Ethelred* commonly known as the "unready" was King of England from 978 to 1016 after the death of his brother Edward the Martyr. Emma or Ælfgifu, dubbed the "gem of the Normans" was the mother of Edward the Confessor by Ethelred, but later married Cnut, and by him was mother of Harthacnut. Her nephew Robert was the father of William the Bastard later King of England.

## Chapter 2:

*Earl Thoret* is otherwise unknown: Aelred may have confused him with Thorkell, a Danish invader who took service under Ethelred and probably became a Christian. *Alfred* may well have been in fact younger than Edward. He foolishly entered England in 1036 and was captured by Godwine and murdered near Guildford. If Edward were the elder and thus the first legitimate son, the choice of him as heir seems less strange.

## Chapter 3:

*Was born* at Islip in 1002.

*To Normandy.* Emma, Alfred and Edward were entrusted to Bishop Ælfhun to escort to Normandy in 1013. Cnut campaigned in England from that date until he secured the throne in 1017. In that year he married Emma, by whom he had Harthacnut who succeeded him in 1035. In consequence her sons Alfred and Edward were disinherited.

## Chapter 4:

*They have poured out...* Psalm 78:3.

*Brithwald*, originally a monk of Glastonbury, was bishop not of Winchester but of Ramsbury from 995 to 1045. There was a local cult of him as a saint, celebrated on 22 January.

*The bishop...asked* Aelred alters the story from the version given by Osbert and William of Malmesbury, in which it was Edward himself who asked St Peter for an oracle, and thus obtained a prophecy about Harold: here Brithwald asks for and obtains information about Edward.

*Your people have sinned...* Aelred, like the author of Chronicles, sees temporal prosperity or disaster as a measure of the sinfulness or otherwise of the nation. This will run him into some difficulties in reconciling Edward's idyllic reign with the depravity of the nation which invited the Norman Conquest.

*When you are asleep.* Actually Brithwald lived three years after the accession of Edward.

## Chapter 5:

*Edmund* was slain in 1016, but he may have died of natural causes. His son Edward the Exile survived to become the father of Edgar the Ætheling and Margaret of Scotland, hence an ancestor of Henry II (see Appendix).

*Crossed to England* Edward may have come with him and attempted to seize the throne.

*Edwin* of Northumbria (585 - 633) was preserved from betrayal by his host in exile at the intervention of Saint Paulinus who afterwards converted him to Christianity.

*Oswald* also of Northumbria (605 - 642) became a Christian while in exile on Iona, and afterwards successfully claimed the throne of his father Æthelfrith.

*Cnut was taken* in 1035. *His sons* were Harold Harefoot, who ruled in northern England and died in 1040, and Harthacnut who ruled at first in Wessex and briefly over all England and Denmark. An elder son, Sweyn, inherited Norway. Harthacnut invited Edward to England in 1041 and recognised him as his heir. He died on 8 June 1042, and Edward was acclaimed immediately as king.

*Consecrated as king* on Easter Sunday, 3rd April 1043, by Eadsige, Archbishop of Canterbury.

*Roman Emperor* Henry III (1039 - 56). His cousin, who was the wife of Edward the Exile, is named elsewhere as Agatha (see Appendix): she may have been the daughter of Saint István of Hungary.

*King of France* Henri I (1031 - 1060).

*All the kings* II Chron. 9:23.

## Chapter 6:

*They have made...* Ecclesiasticus 32:1.

## Chapter 8:

*Earl Godwine* of Wessex, the most powerful magnate in England, was influential in ensuring the succession of Edward but resisted the Norman interest. He had five sons, Swein, Harold, Tostig, Siward and Gurth, who all played significant parts in subsequent events. Raising the standard of revolt, they were exiled in 1051, but invaded the realm in 1052 and forced Edward to reinstate them. Aelred is consistently anti-Godwine.

*Edith* married Edward on 23 January 1045, was banished by him to a convent at Wherwell, not far from Winchester, in 1051 on Godwine's revolt, but reinstated in 1052.

## Chapter 9:

*The Danish King* must have been Magnus, king of Norway, who fought Svein Estrithson, nephew of Cnut, for the Danish crown. He died suddenly in 1047 after which Svein secured the throne.

## Chapter 10:

*His vow* to visit the relics of St Peter in Rome if he were established on the throne of England (chapter 5).

*Aldred* was actually Bishop of Worcester at the time. He was ambassador to the Emperor in 1044, Bishop of Hereford and Ramsbury, and finally Archbishop of York in 1060 (see chapter 14). *Hereman* was bishop of Sherborne. Their expedition took place in 1049 - 1050.

*Pope Leo* is Saint Leo IX (1049 - 1054). The *synod* was either the Easter Synod of 1049, which enforced celibacy of the clergy or that if 1050 which condemned Berengarius. It is unclear which one the English bishops attended.

The *Papal Rescript* is cited in Osbert's *Life of Edward*, probably from a copy preserved at Westminster.

## Chapter 11:

*Thorney* that is Westminster.

*The heavy tax...* this was abolished in 1051. It is supposed to have amounted to £36,000.

*Happy the man...* Ecclesiasticus 31:8.

## Chapter 12:

*St Peter's Abbey* that is Westminster.

## Chapter 13:

*Ethelbert* or Æthelberht of Kent (552 - 616) was St Augustine's convert and patron. *Sebert* of Essex, not East Anglia, supported St *Mellitus* in founding the see of London, and is claimed as founder by both St Paul's and Westminster. He died in 616.

*St Gregory had sent* in 601. Augustine became Archbishop of Canterbury in 619 and died in 624.

*A certain fisherman* traditionally named Edric. His descendants claimed the privilege of presenting a salmon to the abbot every St Peter's day until the late 14th century.

*The pavement inscribed...* this was one of the most significant

129

ceremonies of the consecration of a church, ritually claiming ownership of the land for Christ, the alpha and omega. The walls were anointed in twelve places, marked with crosses and illuminated with candles, symbolising the twelve foundation stones of the heavenly Jerusalem. The imagery comes largely from the Apocalypse.

*The tithe* was received from all the Thames fisheries throughout the life of the abbey.

## Chapter 14:

*Messengers again:* this embassy took place in 1061. Tostig and Harold were also in Rome at the time, and they travelled back together.

*Aldred* was appointed Archbishop of York in 1060 and needed to claim the pallium. This was in fact refused by the Pope, and he was degraded from his episcopate, but afterwards Tostig persuaded the Pope to reinstate him and grant the pallium. He died in 1069. *Giso* bishop of Wells was a reformer, who survived until 1088. *Walter* of Lorraine, Bishop of Hereford, was chaplain to Queen Edith and opposed by William I. He died in 1079.

*The Pope* Nicholas II (1059 - 1061).

*The council* not an ecumenical council but a "Concilium Romanum" which issued a decree against simony, hence the pope's hostility to Aldred.

*With no untoward incident.* On the contrary, they travelled with Tostig, were beset by brigands, robbed and had to creep back to Rome, where they were kindly received and Aldred was reinstated.

*The two letters* are both taken from Osbert.

*Your worthy predecessor* His immediate predecessor was Stephen X, 1057-58, of no importance. The king must be referring to St Leo IX.

*Dedicated himself totally...* other historians say he spent most of his time hunting: William of Malmesbury speaks of his passion for the chase to the exclusion of the interests of the

130

realm (William of Malmesbury, 220).

## Chapter 15:

*Earl Leofric* with Godwine one of the most powerful men in England. He was Earl of Mercia from about 1030 till his death in 1057. His wife *Godgyfu* or Godiva was a benefactress of the city of Coventry.

## Chapter 16:

A similar story is told of Aelred himself (Daniel, p 46-7).
*Fruit of her womb...* William of Malmesbury tells us she had twins (W. of M., 222).

## Chapter 17:

*Gift of healing...* It was common to attribute healing power to the touch of an anointed king, although the limitation of this to scrofula, the "King's Evil", is a later medieval tradition. William of Malmesbury is indignant against those who think St Edward's miracles were performed through the grace inherent in kingship rather than his personal merits (W. of M., 222).

## Chapter 19:

*Brill.* Migne's text says "Bruheham" but Osbert has "Bruhellam" which appears to be Brill in Buckinghamshire. William of Malmesbury names the man Wulfwine, called Spillecorn, son of William of Nutegareshale, i.e. Ludgershall, Bucks. (W. of M., 224).
*The royal palace.* Osbert says this was at Windsor, where there was also a church dedicated to St Peter.

## Chapter 21:

*Tostig was exiled* actually by Edward himself, in 1065, for he had succeeded as Earl of Northumberland in 1054, and had made himself so unpopular that the Northumbrians rose in revolt, choosing Morcar, grandson of Leofric, instead. Tostig took refuge in Flanders, but in 1066 joined Hardrada in the invasion of England which Harold checked at Stamford Bridge, shortly before his own defeat at the hands of William.

## Chapter 22:

*A popular festival*, Easter Monday 1053.

*My brother* Alfred the Ætheling, killed in 1036, probably by Godwine.

*Soon afterwards* Godwine died at Winchester on Easter Thursday, 15th April 1053, following what seems to have been a stroke.

## Chapter 23:

*The Seven Sleepers* of Ephesus were young men who took refuge in a cave during the persecution of Decius (c 250), and were discovered still asleep in the reign of Theodosius II (c 450). Their tomb became a place of pilgrimage, but it was not normally considered that they could be seen still sleeping. Their feast day is 27th July.

*The Emperor* Constantine Monomachus, died 1054.

*Syria was overrun* by the Seljuk Turks in 1071 after the tragic battle of Manzikert.

*The kings...were slain.* Diogenes of Constantinople was deposed and blinded after Manzikert; Henry III of the Western Empire died peacefully in 1086, but was succeeded by the troublesome Henry IV; the King of France, Henri I, died suddenly, possibly by poison, in 1060; and the fate of Harold of England was well known. William of Malmesbury adds other disasters (W. of M. 225).

## Chapter 24:

*A church had been built* said to have been at Clavering in Essex (Stanley, 1869, p 29 n).

*Two men* from Ludlow in Shropshire, represented on a

stained glass window in the church there. (Stanley, 1869, p 29 n).

*The ring* was preserved at Westminster Abbey for many centuries, having been extracted from the tomb of Edward by Abbot Lawrence.

## Chapter 25:

*Holy Innocents' Day.* the Abbey was consecrated on 28th December 1065, by Archbishop Stigand.

## Chapter 26:

The decadence and depravity of the realm accords ill with the idyllic account of Edward's reign in Chapter 5. But perhaps the Godwine family were responsible for all the crimes of England.

*Robert*, probably Robert FitzWimarc, a Norman, "staller" in the court of Edward, and subsequently supporter of William.

*Stigand* was intruded into Canterbury in 1052 after Robert of Jumièges was driven out on the return from exile of Godwine. Despite papal support, Robert was unable to regain his see, and died at Jumièges. Stigand was excommunicated by five popes, before receiving the pallium from the simoniac antipope "Benedict X". He was later deposed (see chapter 33).

## Chapter 27:

*Saint Dunstan* was credited with many visions and prophecies: Aelred may here refer to his warning to Ethelred that wars and destruction would follow his obtaining the kingdom by the shedding of his brother's blood (cited in Porter, 1632, p 456).

Aelred's interpretation of the vision fits neatly into his theme of support for Henry II. Previous authors had simply taken the oracle of the cut tree to represent an impossibility: see Barlow's discussion of this at the end of his edition of the Anonymous *Life*.

## Chapter 28:

*The day before the Nones of January* would put Edward's death on 4th January 1066: it is more usually commemorated on the 5th, which is the date given in the Anglo-Saxon Chronicle. Certainly his funeral, and Harold's coronation, took place on the 6th (See Bloch, 1923, p 111 n).

## Chapter 31:

*Promised on oath* according to the Norman tradition. It does appear that Edward himself had named William as his heir, although commending his queen to Harold might be construed as a way of bequeathing the kingdom as well. In any case the descendants of Edmund Ironside seem to have been passed over.

*Alsinus* otherwise Alxus or Ælfwine.

*Stamford Bridge* the battle took place on 25th September 1066, putting an end to Scandanavian attempts on the English crown.

## Chapter 33:

*A synod...* there were in fact several synods, which Aelred conflates. It was in 1070 that *Stigand* was deposed and replaced by Lanfranc, who ruled Canterbury until 1089 and with William's assistance remodelled the Church in England.

*Wulfstan* was Bishop of Worcester from 1062 until 1095. He was canonised by Pope Innocent III in 1203 and his feastday is 19th January. The story of his deposition and reinstatement seems to originate with Osbert. By 1163 it was sufficiently famous for Becket to ask for the tombstone in which the staff had been fixed as a souvenir of the translation of St Edward's body (Barlow 1970, p 284).

*With this staff invested me.* It was of course the question of royal investiture that was the principle matter of contention between Gregory VII and the Emperor Henry IV, being resolved at the very time of Lanfranc's campaign. It is curious that Aelred, a century later, sees nothing strange in Wulfstan's recognition of Edward's right to invest him with staff and ring.

*Gundulf* was Bishop of Rochester from 1077 to 1108, and was one of Lanfranc's new men.

*A feretory...* this was replaced in the time of Henry III by the shrine, much of which still remains.

## Chapter 34:

*Gilbert Crispin* was abbot of Westminster from 1085 to 1117. The first examination of the body took place in 1102 (Squire 1969, p 93).

## Chapter 35:

*St Edward King and Martyr* the brother of Ethelred, was killed at Corfe in 978. A cult developed around his shrine at Shaftesbury, but it seems unlikely that his feastday (18 March) would have been kept as a day when work was prohibited in London. There is obviously some confusion between the two Saints Edward, and not only in the mind of the apprentice.

## Chapter 36:

*Osbert* is the monk of Westminster who in 1138 wrote the *Life of Edward* which Aelred is rewriting. He was prior of Westminster in 1136, and travelled to Rome in 1141 in an unsuccessful attempt to persuade Pope Innocent II to canonise Edward. He wrote a number of other lives of Anglo-Saxon saints.

## Appendix:

The text appears in Migne's *Patrologia Latina*, vol. cxcv, col. 734. Much of it seems to derive from William of Malmesbury

(c. 228), who states that Edward the Exile was brought home from Hungary, and died in St Paul's Cathedral.

*Agatha* may have been the daughter of King István of Hungary (St Stephen). *Edgar* was twice passed over for the kingship and died in obscurity. *Margaret* as Queen of Scotland perpetuated the Saxon line. *Christina* ended her days as a nun at Romsey. William of Malmesbury goes on to say that Edward the Confessor pledged his throne to William on the death of the Exile, despairing of any other successor.

# Bibliography

*Acta Sanctorum*: Vol. 1, coll. 290 - 305 (5th January), Paris, 1863.

Barlow 1962: *The Life of King Edward who rests at Westminster* edited and translated by Frank Barlow, Nelson Medieval Classics, 1962.

Barlow 1965: 'Edward the Confessor's Early Life, Character and Attitudes', *English Historical Review* CCCXV, April 1965, vol. 80, pp 225 - 251.

Barlow 1970: *Edward the Confessor* by Frank Barlow, London 1970.

Bloch, 1923: 'La Vie de S. Edouard le Confesseur par Osbert de Clare', edited by Marc Bloch, *Analecta Bollandiana* XLI (1923) pp 5 - 131.

Daniel, 1950: *The Life of Ailred of Rievaulx* by Walter Daniel, translated and edited by F.M. Powicke, Nelson Medieval Classics, 1950.

Migne, *Patrologia Latina*, Vol. CXCV, colls. 737 - 790.

Porter, 1632: *The Flowers of the Lives of our English Saincts*, by the R. Father Hierome Porter, O.S.B., vol. I, Doway, 1632, pp 1 - 35 (5th January).

Squire, 1969: *Aelred of Rievaulx* by Aelred Squire O.P., London, 1969.

Stanley 1869: *Historical Memorials of Westminster Abbey*, by Dean A. P. Stanley, London, 1869.

Stenton, 1971: *Anglo-Saxon England* by F.M. Stenton, Oxford History of England Vol II, 1971.

Twysden, 1652: *Historiæ Anglicanæ Scriptores X*, edited by Roger Twysden and introduced by John Selden, London, 1652.

Whitelock 1961: *The Anglo-Saxon Chronicle, A revised*

*Translation*, ed. Dorothy Whitelock, 1961.

William of Malmesbury: *De Gestis Regum Anglorum*, Rolls Series 1887; Vol. I, pp 271-280.